KNOWING YOUR RIGHTS

Taking Back Our Religious Liberties: A Handbook

by

JAY ALAN SEKULOW

ABOUT THE AUTHOR

Jay Alan Sekulow is Chief Counsel for the American Center for Law and Justice. He has won several key Supreme Court decisions protecting the rights of Christians who spread the Gospel to the general public.

A popular public speaker, he has appeared on *Good Morning America, Nightline, Phil Donahue, CNN Crossfire, Larry King Live,* and is a regular guest on *The 700 Club.*

He received his bachelor's degree and his doctor of jurisprudence from Mercer University, where he graduated cum laude and served as an editorial staff member on the Mercer Law Review.

Mr. Sekulow is also the author of *From Intimidation to Victory.*

This exclusive edition of *Knowing Your Rights* is published by The Christian Broadcasting Network, Inc., as a complement to Pat Robertson's book, *The Turning Tide,* published by Word, Inc., October 1993. Illustrations and design by Tom N. Tierney. Edited by Stephen M. Elliott. Any reproduction of this material requires written permission of CBN, Inc.

Copyright © 1993 by Liberty, Life, and Family Publications. All rights reserved.

No part of this publication may be reproduced in any form, or stored in a database or retrieval system, or transmitted or distributed in any form by any means, electronic, mechanical photocopying, recording, or otherwise, without the prior written permission of Liberty, Life, and Family, except as permitted by the Copyright Act of 1976. To secure such permission, write Liberty, Life, and Family, Publications Department, 1000 Thomas Jefferson Street, N.W., Suite 520, Washington, D.C. 20007.

DEDICATION

This book is dedicated to Keith A. Fournier, Esq., Executive Director of the American Center for Law and Justice. Keith's superb management of the American Center has allowed me and our litigation team to do what we are best at — going to court.

ACKNOWLEDGMENTS

This project has been a team effort. I especially want to thank my associate Joel Thornton, whose role has been more of a co-author than a research assistant. James M. Henderson, Sr., who heads up the American Center for Law and Justice's Washington, D.C., office, did an outstanding job on the chapters dealing with evangelism. I also want to thank my associate David Etheriedge for his assistance on the chapters dealing with school issues. Gene Kapp, who is the media director for the American Center for Law and Justice, enabled me to have a section concentrating on utilizing the press. I would be remiss not to mention the diligent work of our editor, William Watkins, who did an exceptional job in making our legal jargon understandable.

TABLE OF CONTENTS

INTRODUCTION

This book is about our freedoms — our constitutionally protected liberties as citizens of the United States. Among these liberties, a most important one is the freedom of speech, which gives us the right to speak out on any issue from a biblical perspective. In the ongoing struggle over the direction of our culture, we dare not lose this right. And yet it, along with many of our other freedoms, is under attack. School administrators, government bureaucrats, special interest groups, even certain legal societies are intimidating Christians into leaving the public arena and exercising their faith only in the private sphere.

But the Constitution has not changed. Like everyone else, Christians still have the right to be heard. The Supreme Court has repeatedly recognized that "Above all else the First Amendment means that government has no power to restrict expression because of its message, its ideas, its subject matter, or its content. For the state to enforce the content-based exclusion it must show that its regulation is necessary to serve a compelling state interest and that it is narrowly drawn to achieve that end."

Attempts to stifle Christian voices generally fail the constitutional tests. However, all too frequently Christians back down at even the first hint of opposition. So although we are winning more in the courts, we cannot afford to retreat from the streets and our halls of government, turning the marketplace of ideas over to those who are ignorant of or even hostile to our faith. We must make sure our voices are being heard where they are needed most, so we do not lose our society to non-Christian worldviews and destructive values.

Our society did not begin this way. Three hundred and seventy years ago a group of Christians left their native England because of religious persecution. The Pilgrims landed at Plymouth Rock after a strenuous trip at sea. When they emerged from the belly of the Mayflower in 1620, there was more than fresh air for their lungs and ample room to stretch their legs. They discovered freedom to believe. Freedom to worship. Freedom to pray as they wished. Freedom to participate in government. Freedoms, I regret to say, we no longer enjoy without stifling interference, whether in the public schools, on city streets, or before city councils. Our freedoms are eroding before our eyes.

We must stop taking our constitutional liberties for granted and take them back. Many Christians are doing just that. Consequently, during the last few years, we have made significant gains in restoring the freedoms of speech, assembly, and the press. The Lord has granted us victories from city courts to the United States Supreme Court. The tide is turning. We dare not, however, become complacent. Now, more than ever, we need to not only defend our rights but go on the offensive. I have written this book so you can join me in doing just that.

As the Chief Counsel for The American Center for Law and Justice, I have received thousands of requests for assistance from people who feel that their rights have been violated. Many of these requests relate to religious expression in the public schools, religious discrimination in the workplace, and the right to share views publicly, whether that means sharing the Gospel or addressing contemporary issues from a biblical viewpoint. In the pages that follow, I provide answers to many of these recurring questions and deal with others as well. My answers are based on general legal principles that may or may not apply to any given situation. Because each actual case is unique, the specific facts of each case have a direct impact on its outcome. So my answers will give you general guidance, but you may need to seek professional legal counsel to address the specifics of your situation.

My heartfelt desire is that this book will help you understand what your rights are and the parameters within which you can exercise these rights. In other words, my goal is that once you understand your rights, you will act on them!

I believe we are on the threshold of major change in our country. But our continued and stepped up involvement is critical to channel the momentum toward true liberty. We can impact our culture for Christ. May this book enable you to become more bold in the marketplace of ideas as you stand on your rights and speak out for Him.

Jay Alan Sekulow
September 1993

Taking the Gospel to the streets is a commission and a commandment for believers. Responding obediently to the Commission and hitting the streets, we receive grace and power to fulfill the Lord's commands. Hitting the streets always has had a personal cost. Consider the price paid by Stephen, who became the first martyr for preaching the Gospel. And remember Peter, James and John, who preached in the name of Jesus, even though threatened with imprisonment.

Today, however, American Christians face no such cost for preaching the Gospel. The streets and sidewalks of the United States are an open forum for evangelism.

Isn't it strange that when the time comes to hit the streets, many Christians with willing hearts hesitate for fear that their preaching may result in arrest and prosecution. True, from time to time those who preach the Gospel are challenged by government officials regarding the use of public streets, parks and sidewalks for evangelism activities. But, as a general rule, such fears are unfounded.

In the following pages, we show

PUBLIC PLACES: Christians In The Marketplace Of Ideas

66The streets and sidewalks of the United States are an open forum for evangelism.99

Taking The Gospel To The Streets

how the Constitution guarantees your right to preach the Gospel in public places. For over 60 years, the Supreme Court has examined cases involving preaching (or other speech activities) on the streets. These cases provide ready answers to those who challenge your right to take the Gospel to the streets.

Q **What do you mean by "taking the Gospel to the streets?"**

A Taking the Gospel to the streets means using written and spoken words to tell the man or woman on the street about Jesus. Taking the Gospel to the streets means giving away tracts, pamphlets, and other printed material that presents the Gospel. Taking the Gospel to the streets means speaking to people on the streets — telling them about the Lord and his free gift of salvation.

Q **What laws protect my right to take the Gospel to the streets?**

A When you give away Gospel tracts in public places — streets, sidewalks and parks — you are engaged in a form of speech and publication protected by the United States Constitution and civil rights laws. When you speak with someone about the Gospel while in a public place, you enjoy constitutional protection.

The laws of this nation and of your state, which protect other forms of speech and press, protect your rights to evangelize. As American citizens, we are protected by the United States Constitution from government interference with our right of free speech. Also, the Constitutions of every state in our country include guarantees of free speech, which are at least as protective of free speech as the American Constitution. Some state constitutions (including California and New Jersey) are more protective of speech than the First Amendment.

The First Amendment to the United States Constitution says: "Congress shall make no law... abridging the freedom of speech...." The Fourteenth Amendment says: "nor shall any State deprive any person of life, liberty, or prosperity, without due process of law...."

The Supreme Court has ruled that these two parts of the Constitu-

> **66 We are protected by the United States Constitution from government interference with our right of free speech. Also, the Constitutions of every state in our country include guarantees of free speech. 99**

tion severely limit the power of federal, state and local governments to interfere with speech activities on sidewalks, streets and in parks.

Q When I have handed out Gospel literature in the past, police have stopped me and told me that soliciting is not allowed. Am I soliciting when I share the Gospel?

A No! Giving away free Gospel tracts and talking to people about salvation are not the same thing as soliciting. The Supreme Court recently decided a case involving the difference between soliciting and leafletting. In the *Kokinda* case, the Supreme Court permitted the postal service to enforce a rule against asking (soliciting) for donations on postal property. In that case, political activists were asking for donations while standing on a sidewalk leading from the post office building to the post office parking lot.

However, the court suggested that it would reject a rule that banned free distribution of literature on such properties. Discussing the difference, the Court said,

2

As residents of metropolitan areas know from daily experience, confrontation by a person asking for money disrupts passage and is more intrusive and intimidating than an encounter with a person giving out information. One need not ponder the contents of a leaflet or pamphlet in order mechanically to take it out of someone's hand, but one must listen, comprehend, decide and act in order to respond to a solicitation.[1]

In the *ISKCON, Inc. v. Lee* and *Lee v. ISKCON, Inc.* cases, the Supreme Court considered a restriction on leafletting and another restriction on solicitation of donations in airport terminals operated by the Port Authority of New York and New Jersey. The Court concluded that, despite the fact that the airport terminals were nonpublic forums, a regulation barring the distribution of free literature in the terminals was unreasonable and unconstitutional. The Court also held that solicitation is separate from literature distribution and can thereby be banned, even though literature distribution cannot be banned.

ISKCON together with *Kokinda* reinforce the concept that solicitation and the distribution of literature are separate. While a city official may, in some instances, not allow solicitation, such a regulation may not be broadened to include literature distribution.

As long as you are giving away your literature for free, and you aren't panhandling for donations, you are engaging in the most protected form of speech. That does not mean that you will never have problems. Although it is often just an excuse for stopping street evangelism, this is one of the objections to leafletting we hear about most frequently. It often takes a strongly worded letter to attorneys for the city or county involved to resolve the problem.

Q Where can I go to hand out Gospel tracts to the public?

A You can go to any publicly owned street, sidewalk or park. In legal terms, streets, sidewalks and parks are "traditional public forums." That means that these are the places people traditionally relate to public speeches or leafletting; we are accustomed to the presence of newspaper boxes and paperboys on public sidewalks; we expect the candidates in an upcoming election to hold their rallies at the park; and we assume that when some group is unhappy about something they are likely to march down a nearby street. None of these activities surprise us. Why? Because streets, sidewalks and parks are traditionally connected in our history and experience to free speech activities.

Sometimes a city official will get confused about these "traditional public forums." For example, in *Frisby v. Schulte* (487 U.S. 474) the Supreme Court rejected a Wisconsin city's argument that the streets and sidewalks of a residential area were not the sort of "traditional public forums" that the Court had held were generally open to free speech and activities. In that case, the Court showed that it was no longer acceptable for governments to make such arguments because, in the Court's view, a street is a street is a street. The Court noted that the kinds of regulations that would be permissible varied with the nature of the streets at issue. For example, a rule against parades between sunset and sunrise on residential streets serves a valid purpose of protecting the peace of a neighborhood during a time when most residents are resting. A rule against a noisy activity on a hospital street or on a street near a school during school hours are other examples of reasonable rules.

You are not limited to streets, parks and sidewalks for tract distribution. Courts have found many other places to be appropriate. Airport terminals and bus and train stations have all been found by courts to be appropriate locations for leafletting. The walkways and sidewalks surrounding government-owned coliseums and stadiums are also appropriate. Many tourist attractions around the country are appropriate locations, as well. For example, the walkways and paths surrounding the Washington Monument and the Vietnam Veterans Memorial are protected.

Q **When witnessing, sometimes I am on a sidewalk in front of a business. I have had police officers tell me that I must move away from a business or that I must keep moving or I will be "loitering." Is this right?**

A No! "Loitering" means that you have no legitimate purpose or business for being in a certain place. But your evangelism activities are a legitimate purpose for standing on a sidewalk. Of course, if you try standing in the middle of the street, you may run into a different problem. (But that problem is obstructing the flow of traffic, not "loitering".) The loitering charge, when made against a street evangelist who is actively preaching the Gospel, is invalid.

Of course, you don't have the right to barricade a sidewalk, allowing only those who will take a tract to pass. Your right to use the sidewalks, streets and parks is not a license to make them unusable for others. Besides, how effective will your preaching be if you anger those around you by treating them rudely or blocking their way?

Q **I don't live in the town where I want to hand out Gospel tracts and preach on the streets. Police tell me that I don't have the same rights when visiting a town or state away from home. Is this right?**

A You are not limited to the streets, sidewalks and parks in your town. Many cases which we have brought involve visitors from other towns or other states. The constitutional rule is that state and local governments cannot treat visitors from out of town or another state differently than local residents.

Q I want to get started witnessing to the Good News of the Gospel. What should I do?

A First, devote time to prayer and prayerful preparation.

Next, select a target. You may choose some particular place because of the opportunity to reach many people — outside a sports stadium or near a historic monument. You may have a target group in mind. For example, if your burden is for young people, you will want to select locations where young people pass by or gather.

If the location you choose is not a nice, simple sidewalk location, you should speak to the appropriate authority to discover what rules have been adopted to govern your activities. (This does not mean that you must always accept, like the Ten Commandments, a rule barring leafletting.) Check with a county clerk, the police department, the security office at the stadium or similar offices. This will let you know what to expect when you witness.

Of course, if you are in a public place and are stopped from distributing free Gospel literature, do not assume that it was correct for you to be stopped. Too many Supreme Court cases have been decided against governments on these matters to assume that government is

> **66 The principle that has emerged from our cases is that the First Amendment forbids the government to regulate speech in ways that favor some viewpoints or ideas at the expense of others. 99**
>
> Opinion of the United States Supreme Court—*Lamb's Chapel v. Center Moriches Union Free School District*, June 7, 1993

always right. Many seemingly hopeless cases in which leafletters ultimately fight will cause many government units to change policies.

Lamb's Chapel And The Use Of Public Facilities

T he victory obtained in the *Lamb's Chapel* case marked an important turning point for Christians obtaining access to the marketplace of ideas. In a unanimous decision, the Court held that religious organizations confronting contemporary issues from a religious perspective cannot be excluded from access to government property available to other groups. No longer can Christians be treated as second-class citizens.[2]

Q What is the *Lamb's Chapel* case?

The facts in the *Lamb's Chapel* case were straightforward. An evangelical church desired to rent a school facility for an evening showing of a film series produced by Dr. James Dobson's Focus on the Family ministry. The film series, entitled "Turn Your Heart Toward Home," dealt with contemporary family issues from a biblical perspective. The church's request for use was denied by school administrators because it was "church related." Although the school facilities were available to community groups for social, civic, and recreational purposes, the rules and regulations specifically prohibited any religious use. The Supreme Court ruled against this prohibition, stating that the religious exclusion was unconstitutional.

Q What is the impact of the *Lamb's Chapel* case?

A In many cities and counties throughout the United States, local school facilities are the town halls of the community. Access to

these town halls is essential for Christians who want to have issues addressed from their perspective. Although many in a community may not feel comfortable going to a church to hear a presentation on a contemporary issue, people do feel at ease attending meetings held in community facilities such as school auditoriums and civic centers. The impact of the *Lamb's Chapel* case is significant. Every government agency, from school boards to city councils, that have access policies in place for their properties must now allow Christians to utilize those facilities as well. We must take advantage of this new openness in the marketplace the *Lamb's Chapel* case has created.

Q Does *Lamb's Chapel* only apply to churches?

A No. Although the particular case before the Supreme Court involved Lamb's Chapel church, now other community groups that want to address issues from a Christian perspective also have access to government facilities that are open to the public for use. For instance, in Mobile, Alabama, an evangelistic ministry known as "Strike Force International" is now entitled to have an evangelistic crusade at the public school in Alabama because of an access policy that had to be modified in light of *Lamb's Chapel*. Evangelistic events can now take place in school facilities in the evening as well as in city halls or other government facilities open to general use.

Q Does *Lamb's Chapel* only apply to school facilities?

A No. The decision in *Lamb's Chapel* applies to *any* government facility, whether a town hall, civic center, or city hall, that is open to the general public for social, civic, or recreational uses. We have found that most cities across America have access policies to local government buildings for community use. We have also found that most of these cities specifically prohibit religious groups from utilizing these facilities. This religious exclusion is unconstitutional in light of the *Lamb's Chapel* decision.

Q What topics can be discussed when using government facilities?

A In *Lamb's Chapel*, the Supreme Court specifically noted that the purpose of the James Dobson film series was to address contemporary family issues from a Christian perspective. But the decision goes much further. Family issues, baccalaureate services for students, evangelistic events, and discussion of contemporary Christian issues can now take place in government facili-

> **66** By inviting the public to attend meetings where our view is presented, we gain access to an important arena where ideas compete for minds and hearts. This is where we need to be. **99**

ties because of the decision in *Lamb's Chapel*. No longer can the excuse of church/state separation be utilized to prohibit Christians from obtaining access to this new marketplace for the presentation of ideas.

Q What about policies that still prohibit use of government facilities by Christians?

A It is time for Christians to go on the offensive and have our voices heard. This will require utilizing the rights that we just obtained from the Supreme Court decision. Unfortunately, many cities are slow to change, and there are still hundreds of policies on the books throughout the United States which specifically prohibit religious groups from utilizing government facilities that are open to the community at large. At The American Center for Law and Justice, we have undertaken a project to have these laws removed and modified so they conform with *Lamb's Chapel*.

The procedure to gain access to a public facility is straightforward. First, if you decide you are going to utilize facilities, you must fill out an application form that is available at the seat of the local city government. Be forthright in the application, and state specifically what purpose you are going to utilize the facilities for. If the policy still prohibits religious uses, ask the city administrators if they are familiar with the *Lamb's Chapel* case. If they are not, we would be happy to send a letter on your behalf to clarify for the city government what the decision in the Supreme Court means. If you continue to have problems gaining access, we have sent demand letters — letters which state the law and inform the city officials what they must do to comply with the law — to city officials in order to obtain access. Generally, the demand letter resolves the situation. However, if we find that the demand letter is being ignored and your rights are still being denied, we can then proceed immediately to federal court and obtain an injunction, which will require the city officials to allow you to utilize the facilities under their control.

We have already seen the fruit from the decision in *Lamb's Chapel*. As I said, in Alabama the *Lamb's Chapel* decision made it possible for an evangelistic event for teenagers to proceed in a local school facility. In Wisconsin, an organization that wanted to present a six-part series on the Christian heritage of our nation was also allowed to meet after the *Lamb's Chapel* decision came down. By utilizing government facilities and inviting the public to attend meetings where our view is presented, we gain access to an important arena and marketplace where ideas compete for minds and hearts. This is where we need to be, carrying Christianity into the fray where it can go head-to-head with other world views and demonstrate its intellectual and practical superiority.

> **66 Even such laws as those barring obstructions or excessive noise are closely reviewed by courts to ensure that 'in the guise of regulation' the government does not seek to 'abridge or deny' such rights. 99**

Picketing And Demonstrating

The following questions address the right to demonstrate in the specific context of the abortion industry. Other citizen-activist groups can apply the principles discussed (for example, as they consider expressing their opposition to the sales and distribution of pornographic materials). A prominent example of such citizen outcry outside the abortion context was the national wave of public protests against the theatrical release of the movie "The Last Temptation of Christ."

The city where we live has an abortion business in it. Our local right-to-life group has developed a public information campaign to make our community aware of the nature of that business. As part of our campaign, we will be going to the public streets and sidewalks near the abortion business to express our opposition to abortion and to share life-giving alternatives to abortion with the business patrons. We have a few questions about this plan:

Q **May we express our opposition to abortion and offer alternatives to it by going personally to the public areas around the business's locale?**

A Yes. You may express your views about abortion while in the vicinity of abortion businesses. There are some important points to bear in mind when engaged in such activities.'

Remember that there is a legal difference between the streets, sidewalks and parks of a community, and the private property owned by another citizen. A key difference is that streets, sidewalks and parks, including those located near abortion businesses, have historically been a place where citizens gather to discuss and debate issues of public importance. The Supreme Court has said that streets, sidewalks and parks "have immemorially been held in trust for the use of the public and, time out of mind, have been used for purposes of assembly, communicating thoughts between citizens, and discussing public questions."[3] So, to stay within the bounds of the law, your activities must occur on the publicly owned streets, sidewalks and parks.

Bear in mind that your city council or county commission can regulate, in certain narrow and specific ways, the time, place, and manner of such activities. For example, a city may enforce a rule against obstructing passage on a public sidewalk or against excessive noise. The Supreme Court has said that the right to engage in expressive activities in public places is not an absolute right and that it "must be exercised in . . . peace and good order."[4] Because rights to freedom of speech, press, and assembly are supremely precious, even such laws as those barring obstructions or excessive noise are closely reviewed by courts to ensure that "in the guise of regulation" the government does not seek to "abridge or deny" such rights.[5]

Q **We are planning a march around the city block where the abortion business is located. We expect more than 100 participants. When we spoke to the city manager's office, we were told that we had to apply for a permit to engage in this activity. Do we have to obtain a permit?**

Perhaps. As noted above, cities can impose reasonable regulations of time, place and manner on speech activities. The Supreme Court has held that the requirement of a permit for a parade or march can be just such a reasonable regulation of speech. At the same time, the Supreme Court has held that governments which impose a requirement of prior permission have imposed a "prior restraint" on speech. Cities that impose such "prior restraints" bear a heavy burden to justify their use. For example, in one recent case, the Supreme Court struck down a parade permit rule because the rule allowed the city to impose greater costs on marches by persons expressing unpopular views.[6]

You should check with the police department or the city manager's office for information on, and a copy of, any ordinance affecting the right to conduct a demonstration or march. If the requirements set out in such ordinances seem burdensome or inappropriate, seek out legal counsel on whether the ordinance is constitutional.

Q We also plan to distribute written materials on abortion. We have been told that we are not allowed to solicit in this manner and that we cannot distribute leaflets because of the litter that results. Do we have the right to distribute literature while we are on the public streets and sidewalks?

Yes. You have the right, in almost every circumstance conceivable, to distribute written materials which express your views on any issue, including abortion. Some misguided bureaucrats may presume that, by calling the distribution of pamphlets "solicitation," they will be able to undermine your right to leaflet. But the Supreme Court has treated leafletting as an activity distinct from solicitation. Leafletting is a well-established model of protected expression. It is a constitutional axiom that distributing written materials in public is a protected exercise of the rights of freedom of speech and press.[7] The Supreme Court has said that, unlike other activities such as oral solicitations for money or business, the distribution is an unobtrusive form of communication.[8]

If you have experienced evangelistic or political literature distribution, then you know, as do thousands of "residents of metropolitan areas[, that] confrontation by a person asking for money disrupts passage and is more intrusive and intimidating than an encounter with a person giving out information."[9] Leafletting is unobtrusive because the recipient "need not ponder the contents of a leaflet or pamphlet in order mechanically to take it out of someone's hand . . . ."[10]

Nor may your city justifiably treat leafletting as a crime. Long ago, the Supreme Court declared unconstitutional a city ordinance which prohibited leafletting in order to prevent the problems associated with litter.[11] A city's desire to keep the streets clean and the sewers unclogged, the Supreme Court has said, "is insufficient to justify an ordinance which prohibits a person rightfully on a public street from handing literature to one willing to receive it."[12] Rather than silencing those who are exercising the constitutional rights to freedom of speech and of the press, your city must address its fears about litter by punishing those who litter, not those who leaflet.

66 Unless you are the government or its representative, you cannot violate the Establishment Clause of the First Amendment. Private persons cannot violate the Establishment Clause. 99

Organizing National Day Of Prayer Rallies

On the National Day of Prayer, I would like to coordinate a public prayer service on the plaza in front of the county courthouse and government center. I know this area has been used for arts festivals, craft fairs, and political campaign events, among other things. When I requested to use the plaza for an hour-long prayer service, my request was denied. I was told that "separation of church and state" would be violated if prayer were permitted on the county-owned plaza. I have some questions:

Q **Will I violate the Establishment Clause of the Constitution if I sponsor a prayer service on the National Day of Prayer on the courthouse plaza?**

A No. Unless you *are* the government or its representative, you cannot violate the Establishment Clause. On its face, the Establishment Clause only restricts the United States Congress from making laws "respecting an Establishment of Religion." The Supreme Court has interpreted another part of the Constitution, the Fourteenth Amendment, to impose the same limitations on state governments which the Establishment Clause imposes on Congress. But the Supreme Court has never held, nor could it sensibly hold, that private persons can violate the Establishment Clause.

Moreover, when your county government bars you from using a public place, such as the courthouse plaza, because of the religious nature of your planned activity, your county is violating the Establishment Clause by showing hostility toward religion. If the plaza is open for public use and access, and if the plaza has been used for such things as art festivals, craft fairs, and political campaign events, then the county is barred from discriminating against your event because of religion.

Q **In other communities, there isn't an open public space appropriate for the prayer service. Some of these towns have meeting rooms in public libraries or in government office buildings. Can we have access to such public meeting rooms?**

A Yes. In June 1993, the Supreme Court held that a New York school district violated the right to freedom of speech of a church and a pastor when it refused their request to use a school auditorium to publicly show a film series on contemporary family issues.[13] The school district directly stated that it was the religious nature of the planned activity that led to the denial of permission. The school district argued that its denial of a religious use of the public facilities under its control was necessary to avoid a violation of the Establishment Clause. The Supreme Court held that the school district had engaged in prohibited viewpoint discrimination. Based on the Supreme

Court's holding, and assuming in your case that such public meeting rooms are open to citizen use for the purpose of discussing public issues of importance, there is no justifiable basis for excluding an event because of its religious nature.

66 The Supreme Court has never said that private citizens can be barred from setting up a nativity display, or any other display of a religious nature, in a public park. 99

Rights Regarding Public Nativity Scenes

So many of the activities during the Christmas season have become completely secularized. Our church would like to help "Keep Christ In Christmas" by erecting a nativity scene in a popular park here in town. Here are some questions we have about this.

Q Didn't the Supreme Court rule a few years ago that such nativity displays are unconstitutional?

A No. The Supreme Court has never said that private citizens can be barred from setting up a nativity display, or any other display of a religious nature, in a public park. In the only two cases decided by the Supreme Court, the nativity displays were either owned or maintained and promoted by the government.[14] In one case, the nativity display, which was part of a larger display with a generally secular theme, was held not to violate the Establishment Clause.[15] In the other case, the nativity display, which stood alone, was held to be a violation of the Establishment Clause.[16]

Q Can the parks department compel us to include such things as snowmen, fairies, Santa Clauses, etc., in order to emphasize secular aspects of the holiday? Can they bar us from including such wholly religious aspects as a sign saying "Keep Christ In Christmas?"

> **" Think of your nativity display as a message to the public. Viewed this way, it becomes clear that it is inappropriate and unconstitutional for a government entity to meddle with your message."**

Q Can they prohibit us from singing traditional religious Christmas music? Can they compel us to sing secular songs?

A No. No. No. No. In order to understand the legal issues involved, think of your nativity display as a message to the public. By setting up the creche, you are telling your fellow citizens to "Keep Christ In Christmas." By singing traditional, religious carols, you are showing the public how to "Keep Christ In Christmas."

Viewed in this way, it becomes clear that it is inappropriate and unconstitutional for a government entity to meddle with your message. Fifty years ago, the United States Supreme Court held that a religious adherent could not be compelled to participate in a flag salute if such participation would violate rights of conscience.[17] Compelling a flag salute in such circumstances would be a presumption that a government official could prescribe orthodoxy of opinion. But, as the Supreme Court interpreted the Constitution, such a presumption was unconstitutional. The Supreme Court said, "[i]f there is any fixed star in our constitutional constellation, it is that no official, high or petty, can prescribe what shall be orthodox in politics, nationalism, religion, or other matters of opinion or force citizens to confess by word or act their faith therein."[18] In like manner, a parks authority official cannot determine for you what kind of expression is appropriate in your private display.

> ❝ Those who have thrown off moral restraint have misused the First Amendment's protection of free speech to justify the production and sale of even the most vile and violent pornography. ❞

Removing Pornography From Your Community

C ommunities have the right to regulate pornography according to local standards. That means they can restrict what is sold, where it is sold, and who is able to buy it. They can even prohibit pornography altogether.

Finding out who is carrying pornography is an important step toward eradicating it. Targeting convenience stores selling adult magazines, video stores renting adult movies, gift stores selling pornographic novelty items, and any other merchant that is selling sexually explicit material can be an effective way of eliminating pornography from a community. What I mean by targeting is the exercise of our First Amendment freedom of speech and freedom of assembly rights so our voices are heard.

Distributing literature, peaceful protests and picketing in objection to the materials sold in the stores are proven techniques for removing pornography. Another way of removing pornography is to stand with a camera in front of stores selling explicit pornographic materials. Many people who frequent these stores do not want their presence documented. You must understand that these particular methods could lead to explosive situations, so never protest or picket alone.

Many groups have organized boycotts through their local churches aimed at merchants selling pornographic materials. Some community activists have gone directly to the city attorney and expressed concern about pornography in the community. City attorneys have several options. First, many cities have ordinances restricting pornography and have simply failed to enforce them. By confronting city attorneys you may find that tough ordinances are already on the books and can be enforced to prohibit unlawful activity. Second, if your community lacks ordinances concerning pornography, talk with city council members about drafting appropriate laws. Other cities have done this and have been very successful in regulating and eliminating pornography. Finally, stores that sell pornographic materials can be zoned into certain areas so the materials are inaccessible to children.

National boycotts have also been effective against convenience store chains that stock soft-core pornographic magazines and against companies that advertise objectionable magazines. Do not simply refrain from patronizing these stores and manufacturers; but actually write to them. Let them know that you cannot, in good conscience, spend your money at their outlets unless they break ties with the pornography they are selling.

National boycotts have been effective tools with network televi-

> **66 By exercising your rights within the guidelines of the First Amendment, your community could be one of those that rises up and halts the flow of filth inside its borders. 99**

sion also. Let the networks know, either by letter or phone call, which shows offend you. Those who control what is being seen on the television screen may not be concerned at all about your morals, but they need you and thousands like you as viewers if they expect to keep ratings high enough to draw sufficient advertising dollars.

Those who have thrown off moral restraint have misused the First Amendment's protection of free speech to justify the production and sale of even the most vile and violent pornography to anyone who wants it — anywhere and at any time. But we do not have to bend to their demands. We can take action to eradicate pornography from our communities. The fight against pornography is really a community fight. By exercising your rights within the guidelines of the First Amendment, your community could be one of those that rises up and halts the flow of filth inside its borders.

STUDENTS' RIGHTS OF FREE SPEECH

The Supreme Court has consistently upheld the rights of students to express themselves on public school campuses. In 1969 the Supreme Court held that students have the right to speak and express themselves on campus. Then in 1990, in the *Westside Community Board of Education v. Mergens* decision, the Court held that Bible clubs and prayer groups can meet on public secondary school campuses. This case interprets the Equal Access Act which Congress passed in 1984 to insure that high school students were not discriminated against in the public schools because of their religious beliefs. The following is a brief look at what the Supreme Court decision means to the American Christian student.

The Supreme Court's decision in *Mergens* is a chance for students to share the Gospel with their peers. It is also a sign of the times. Changes are occurring around us daily. The Gospel cannot be stopped. This Supreme Court decision is an answer to the prayers of God's people across our nation and around our world. This 8-1 decision is a clear message to the country that the time is ripe for action.

> **"The Constitution does not demand that religion be kept out of our public schools. The Constitution only prohibits school sponsored religious activities."**

Rights On Campus

The American Center for Law and Justice receives thousands of inquiries concerning students' rights in public schools. What follows is a brief response to the most commonly asked questions:

Q What does a Supreme Court decision mean?

A A Supreme Court decision has several meanings in our system of government. The one we are concerned with is the decision's effect on our laws as they affect our public high schools. A decision is binding on all lower courts, both federal and state. This means that they must follow the Supreme Court ruling when the facts are similar. There is no appeal from the Supreme Court. When the Supreme Court rules in a case it becomes the law of the land.

Q Does the Constitution actually require that the "separation of church and state" keep religion out of the public schools?

A No! First, the Constitution never mentions the phrase

"separation of church and state." That phrase was first used by Thomas Jefferson in an address to the Danbury Baptist Association in 1802, 13 years after the Constitution was written and accepted as the law of the United States. Neither is the phrase recorded in the notes of the Constitutional Convention. The constitution does say: "Congress shall make no law respecting an establishment of religion, or prohibiting the free exercise thereof[.]" In fact, the Court has said, on numerous occasions, that separation is impossible. Therefore, the Constitution does not demand that religion be kept out of our public schools. The Constitution only prohibits school-sponsored religious activities. Free Exercise of Religion is our right under the Constitution.

> **❝ If a State refused to let religious groups use facilities open to others, then it would demonstrate not neutrality but *hostility* toward religion. ❞**
>
> *Westside Community Schools v. Mergens,* 496 U.S. 226 (1990).

(Bible clubs also includes prayer groups) to meet on campus during non-instructional time. As Justice O'Connor held speaking for the Court in *Mergens,* "[I]f a State refused to let religious groups use facilities open to others, then it would demonstrate not neutrality but *hostility* toward religion."[19]

The way that our educational system is set up, almost all public secondary schools receive federal funds. This means that if the school has clubs that are allowed to meet on campus that are not a part of a class that is being taught, or are not directly related to a school class, then the school must allow your Bible club the same privilege. In other words, the school must give the Bible club or prayer group official recognition on campus. If the school allows service type clubs, such as Interact, Zonta, or 4-H, or clubs like a chess club, it must allow Bible clubs.

Q What did the Supreme Court say in the *Mergens* Bible Club Case?

A In the *Mergens* Bible Club case, the Supreme Court ruled that public secondary schools that receive federal funds and allow non-curriculum related clubs to meet on campus must also allow Bible clubs

Q Can the Bible Club advertise on campus?

A Yes! Once the Bible club is officially recognized it must be allowed to use the public address system, the school bulletin boards, the school newspaper, and take part in club fairs. Thus, the students can use any form of media available to the other clubs to get the message to the rest of the school.

> " Students have the right to discuss religion during class time. Student behavior that is not illegal or disruptive cannot be stopped simply because the particular message is offensive to school officials. "

Bible club in any way. The Bible clubs must be allowed to meet either before school or after school or during a club period with any other clubs. The clubs have a right not only to meet, but also to reach other students with the message that the Bible clubs are meeting.

Q Does this mean that students can now start or attend a Bible club in their public school?

A Yes! The Supreme Court has opened the door for **student-initiated** Bible clubs. The church cannot enter the school and start an outreach program. Students, however, can now begin their own Christian clubs which have any agenda the students desire. The schools must allow students the freedom to actually start or attend their own meetings on the high school campus where the student attends school.

Q Did the Supreme Court limit the rights of Bible clubs in any way?

A No! The Supreme Court did not limit the rights of Bible clubs in any way. Bible clubs must be treated like any other club in the school with full rights and privileges. The school cannot limit the

Q Are the rights of public high school students limited on campus?

A The public high school's mission is to educate students so that they can become productive members of our society. When students do not disrupt the mission of the school they have the same rights as other citizens of the United States. Students even have the right to discuss religion during class time, when religion is a relevant topic. Student behavior that is not illegal or disruptive cannot be stopped by the schools simply because the particular message is offensive to school officials.

Q Can students bring their Bibles to school or wear a Christian shirt?

A Yes! There is no law that prohibits a student from bringing a Bible on campus with him. The student is only bound by an obligation not to "materially or substantially disrupt school discipline."[20] If the student brings his Bible or wears his Christian shirt, the school cannot force the student to remove the shirt or the Bible. Shirts with a message are a form of free speech protected by the First Amendment. *Mergens* clarifies that student speech cannot be discriminated against on campus because of its content.

> **❝ Students do not shed their constitutional rights to freedom of speech or expression at the schoolhouse gate. ❞**
>
> U.S. Supreme Court, *Tinker v. Des Moines Independent School District*, 1969

Q Can public school students share their faith on their campus?

A Yes! In Mergens, the Court reinforced students' rights to evangelize on the high school campus. When we combine *Mergens* with *Tinker v. Des Moines* we find that students' rights are fully protected. Now students can express their First Amendment rights and enjoy the freedom of religion on high school campuses across the country. School officials do not have the right to control student speech just because the particular speech is religious in nature. Students have the right to pass out papers and tracts that are Christian to their peers on campus. As long as the students do not disrupt school discipline, school officials must allow them to be student evangelists. It was argued that to allow the students to meet on campus and to act as student evangelists would violate the Establishment Clause of the First Amendment. This argument was rejected by the Court in *Mergens*. Thus, *Mergens* is a great victory for Christian high school students in America. With the decision in *Mergens*, the Supreme Court has sent a clear message to the school systems of America. No longer will religious discrimination be tolerated under the guise of "separation of church and state."

Q What does this mean to junior high school students?

A The *Mergens* case deals with public secondary schools only (grades 9-12). It is interpreting the Equal Access Act which was passed by Congress and concerns high school students. One of the key questions in *Mergens* was the maturity of high school students as compared to college students. The Court held that high school students were mature enough to distinguish between school-sponsored activities and student-initiated activities. The Court has not yet looked to the junior high school students' ability to make the same distinction.

Q What rights do I have on campus during the school day?

A In *Tinker*, the Supreme Court held that "students [do not] shed their constitutional rights to freedom of speech or expression at the schoolhouse gate."[21] This means that students have the right to express their religious beliefs during the school day. "When [a student] is in the cafeteria, or on the playing field, or on the campus during the authorized hours, he may express his opinions."[22] If school officials refuse to allow you to pray on campus they are censoring your speech and denying your constitutional rights.

Tinker held that students retain their First Amendment rights when they are rightfully on a public school campus. The one limitation the Court placed on the rights of the students is simple: students must not "materially or substantially disrupt school discipline."[23] Thus, as long as students do not disrupt the school they have the right to pray on campus, even around the flagpole.

The nature of public schools does not justify the forfeiture of constitutional rights. In fact, the nature of public schools should enhance the constitutional rights of students and teachers. The school is to teach the student how the laws of the land apply. What better place for a real-life lesson on freedom of speech and religion?

Q What happens now?

A Now the battle begins. The Court has given Christians the right to gather together in public schools. We must begin to use the right we have been given. If the Supreme Court allows us to meet and we fail to meet, what good comes of the right? Like a muscle, our rights must be exercised or they will disappear again. God has opened up a huge mission field. Our missionaries to this field must be our high school students. They can reach their generation for Jesus. They need your support. Pray that the Lord will send laborers to work the fields of the harvest in this hour of great need. God has opened a door. We must walk through it!

Q What if my local high school refuses to allow students to meet or hand out literature on their campus in spite of the *Tinker* and *Mergens* decisions?

A The American Center for Law and Justice is undertaking a national campaign to protect students' freedoms of speech, religion and assembly. We are going to make sure that the *Mergens* decision is obeyed by local school boards. We will institute legal proceedings, when appropriate, to ensure the compliance of school boards with the Court's holding in *Mergens*. (Note: see Appendix I for a detailed legal briefing on students rights.)

> **" A majority of students can do what the State acting on its own cannot do to incorporate prayer in public high school graduation ceremonies. "**
>
> Opinion of the Federal Appeals Court—
> *Jones v. Clear Creek Independent School District*, (1993)

Graduation And Other School Events

Q Can we have student-led prayer at graduation?

A Yes! In *Lee v. Weisman*, the Supreme Court held *only* that it violates the Establishment Clause for *school officials* to *invite clergy* to give prayers at commencement.[24] Justice Kennedy made clear, for the majority, that the Court's decision was limited to the particular facts before the Court.[25] Thus, any change from the factual situation presented in *Lee* might alter the resulting opinion from the Court.

Indeed, following Lee, at least one Federal Appeals Court has ruled that "a majority of students

can do what the State acting on its own cannot do to incorporate prayer in public high school graduation ceremonies."[26] In *Jones v. Clear Creek Independent School District* (Jones II), a post-*Lee* decision, the Fifth Circuit upheld the constitutionality of a school district resolution permitting high school seniors to include a student-led invocation in their graduation ceremony if the majority of the class so votes.[27] Quite unlike the school-directed and school-controlled practice found unconstitutional in *Lee*, the Clear Creek Independent School District's resolution simply permits the students of each graduating class to decide if they do or do not wish to have an invocation as a part of their commencement. In the event that students choose to include an invocation, the resolution provides that it shall be nonsectarian and non-proselytizing and conducted only by a student volunteer.

The *Jones II* Court recognized, as the Supreme Court has previously held, that "there is a crucial difference between government speech endorsing religion, which the Establishment Clause forbids, and private speech endorsing religion, which the Free Speech and Free Exercise Clauses protect."[28]

The Fifth Circuit is the only United States Court of Appeals to have addressed the rights of students to initiate prayers at graduation following the Supreme Court's decision in *Lee v. Weisman*. On June 7, 1993, the Supreme Court denied certiorari in *Jones II*. In other words, the Supreme Court let stand the Fifth Circuit Court of Appeals' decision permitting student-initiated prayer at graduation. Thus, the Fifth Circuit's opinion in *Jones II* provides school boards across the nation, both in and outside the Fifth Circuit, with a valid legal basis for choosing to uphold the rights of students to initiate prayers at graduation.[29]

Some may suggest that school officials should aggressively censor all student expression simply because it occurs within the jurisdiction of the school. The law regarding the First Amendment rights of students is well-established, however. Student speech cannot be restricted because of the content of that speech.

Q Can valedictorians, salutatorians, or honorary student speakers give speeches on religious subjects, including reading from the Bible?

A Yes! As stated previously, it is well-settled that religious speech is protected by the First Amendment of the Constitution.[30] The Supreme Court has firmly held that school administrators can only

> **❝ Where students have been granted freedom to compose their own speeches (e.g., valedictorian or salutatorian addresses, etc.), student expression should not be subjected to censorship because of its content. ❞**

prohibit protected speech by students when it "materially and substantially interfere[s] with the requirements of appropriate discipline in the operation of the school."[31]

Where students have been granted freedom to compose their own speeches (e.g., valedictorian or salutatorian addresses, etc.), or even their own commencement exercise, protected student expression should not be subjected to censorship because of its content. In fact, it is a fundamental proposition of constitutional law that a governmental body may not suppress or exclude the speech of private parties for the sole reason that the speech contains a religious perspective.[32] To deny this bedrock principle would be to undermine the essential guarantees of free speech and religious freedom under the First Amendment.

There is quite a difference between refusing to direct prayer or invite clergy to give prayer at graduation, and choosing to prohibit individual student expression based on its content. The First Amendment precludes any governmental effort to single out and censor — or otherwise burden — the speech of private parties solely because that speech is religious.[33]

A decision by a school board to respect the free speech rights of students and to refrain from censoring student speech based solely on its content is not a deliberate violation of the law. As the Supreme Court has emphasized, students' free speech rights apply even "when [a student] is in the cafeteria, or on the playing field, or on campus during authorized hours . . . ."[34] Students do not "shed their constitutional rights to freedom of speech or expression at the schoolhouse gate."[35] The same axiom is true at graduation.

> **❝ Any official moment of silence must be motivated by a well-defined secular purpose and be neutral on its face, leaving the use of the "moment of silence" to individuals and the dictates of their own conciences. ❞**

Q Can we have Baccalaureate services?

A Yes! Students, community groups and area churches are entitled to sponsor events, such as baccalaureate services. If school facilities are available to the community for use, these groups must be allowed to use school facilities also, regardless of the religious nature of their activities. A policy of equal access for religious speech conveys a message "of neutrality rather than endorsement; if a State refused to let religious groups use facilities open to others, then it would demonstrate not neutrality but hostility toward religion."[36] The United States District Court for the District of Wyoming recently issued a preliminary injunction which allowed a baccalaureate service in a public high school. The court relied directly on *Lamb's Chapel*.[37]

Q Are official "Moments of Silence" permissible under current law?

A Yes! The Supreme Court reviewed the issue of official "moments of silence" in *Wallace v. Jaffree*.[38] While it is true that the Supreme Court did find the *particular* "moment of silence" statute before the Court in that case unconstitutional, the *Wallace* Court did *not* declare that *all* "moments of silence" violate the Establishment Clause. In fact, a majority of the *Wallace* Court clearly recognized that moments of silence are constitutionally permissible: "I agree fully with Justice O'Connor's assertion that some moment-of-silence statutes may be constitutional, a suggestion set forth in the Court's opinion as well."[39] Furthermore, all parties in the *Wallace* case agreed that an Alabama statute mandating a "moment of silence" during classtime was constitutional.[40] *Wallace* held only that the particular facts of the case made the Alabama statute calling for a moment of silence "for meditation *or voluntary prayer*" during classtime unconstitutional.[41] Specifically, the Court focused on the clearly religious intent expressed by the statute's sponsors in the recorded legislative history, and the express language of the statute which called for a moment of silence "for meditation *or voluntary prayer*."[42]

After *Wallace*, it is clear that any official moment of silence must be motivated by a well-defined secular purpose and be neutral on its face, leaving the use of the "moment of silence" to individuals and the dictates of their own consciences.

Q Do students have a right to pray together at school and participate in events like the See You at the Pole National Day of Prayer?

A Yes! See You at the Pole National Day of Prayer is a student-led and student-initiated event. On an annual basis, students across the nation gather with like-minded peers around the flagpole at their respective schools before the class day begins and pray for their schools, teachers, administrators and country.

As discussed in earlier sections, students retain their constitutional rights of free speech and expression, including the right to pray and share personal beliefs, while on their public school campuses. Under the *Tinker* standard, school officials may restrict protected student speech only if it "materially and substantially interfere[s] with appropriate discipline."[43] Thus, school officials may not prevent students from gathering together for prayer and religious discussion on school grounds, provided that students do so in a non-disruptive manner during non-instructional time. Non-instructional time would be immediately before and after school, at lunchtime, or any other "free" time when students are permitted to talk and mingle with peers on campus.

It should be noted that while school officials may not prevent students from engaging in protected religious expression unless it "materially and substantially interferes with

> **" Prayer is a protected form of speech that cannot be banned by school officials when it is being offered in a manner such as See You At The Pole."**

school discipline,"[44] they may impose reasonable time, place and manner restrictions. Such restrictions, however, must be content neutral, "narrowly tailored to serve a significant government interest, and leave open ample alternative channels of communication."[45]

> 66 **When told to prepare an essay on a topic of choice, a student may select the birth of Christ, or any other religious topic the student wishes.** 99

advertise the Prayer Rally. Students must be allowed to use the same forms of advertisement that the other clubs are allowed to use. That includes the public address system, the school bulletin boards, and the school newspaper.

Q Can a See You At The Pole rally be held even if it is not part of an officially recognized club on campus?

A Yes! *Tinker* stands for students' rights to freedom of speech and expression. As long as the activity being participated in does not "materially or substantially interfere with school discipline" students have the right to gather together on campus for prayer, even if no prayer group or Bible club is officially recognized on their campus.

Prayer is a protected form of speech that cannot be banned by school officials when it is being offered in a manner such as See You At The Pole. School officials refusing students the right to pray on their campus is nothing short of censorship.

If there is an officially recognized Bible Club or Prayer Group on campus, then students in the club can

Q Is it constitutional to have holiday observances in the public schools?

A Yes! Students, of course, are free to express their beliefs and convictions as they apply to particular holidays, provided they do so in a non-disruptive manner. (See the discussion of students' rights and *Tinker*, above and in Appendix I.) For example, students have the right to distribute Christmas cards or religious tracts on the "true meaning of Christmas" to their peers during non-instructional time. Students could also wish their classmates a "Merry Christmas" or a "Happy Hanukkah." School officials could not constitutionally prohibit such activities. Further, students may express their individual beliefs during classroom discussions, as well as in the context of *appropriate* class assignments. For instance, an elementary student

26

when instructed to draw a "Thanksgiving" picture may choose to draw a picture of a pilgrim praying to God. Or, when told to prepare an essay on a topic of choice, a student may select the birth of Christ, or any other religious topic the student wishes. School officials cannot discriminate against a student's work simply because of its religious nature.

Regarding official public school observance of religious holidays, an issue separate and distinct from protected student expression, the Eighth Circuit has held that religious songs and symbols can be used in the public schools if they are presented in a "prudent and objective manner and only as part of the cultural and religious heritage of the holiday."[46] The *Florey* Court also stated that the study and performance of religious songs is constitutional if the purpose is the "advancement of the students' knowledge of society's cultural and religious heritage, as well as the provision of an opportunity for students to perform a full range of music, poetry, and drama that is likely to be of interest to the students and their audience."[47]

The *Florey* decision was based

> **❝ In *Stone v. Graham,* the Supreme Court said, "the Bible may constitutionally be used in an appropriate study of history, civilization, ethics, comparative religion, or the like.❞**

largely on a United States Supreme Court opinion: *School District of Abington Township v. Schempp,*[48] In *Schempp,* the Supreme Court said, "It certainly may be said that the Bible is worthy of study for its literary and historic qualities. Nothing we have said here indicates that such study of the Bible or of religion, when presented objectively as part of a secular program of education, may not be effected consistently with the First Amendment."[49]

Q Can the Bible be used as part of the curriculum of the school?

A Yes! In *Stone v. Graham,* the Supreme Court said, "the Bible may constitutionally be used in an appropriate study of history, civilization, ethics, comparative religion, or the like."[50] Thus, it would be constitutional for a public school teacher to have students study the biblical passages that relate to Christmas (e.g., Matthew 1:18-2:22 and Luke 2:1-20) if the purpose was to study the historical or literary significance of the passages. Of course, any student that had ideological or religious objections to reading the Bible should be excused from the assignment.

In addition, the Bible was an important book in the early history of this country. It is possible to set up a curriculum that evaluates the role of the Bible in this country and western civilization that is constitutional. The Bible is also considered to be literature from antiquity. A school board could establish a policy that allows the Bible to be discussed as part of a literature program in the school.

> **" School districts are under no constitutional obligation to rename "Christmas vacation" as "Winter vacation" or some similar name. Any suggestion to the contrary is simply unnecessary and should be avoided. "**

speakers from public schools in *Lamb's Chapel*. In refusing to uphold a religious exclusion, the *Lamb's Chapel* Court states that "the principle that has emerged from our cases is that the First Amendment forbids the government to regulate speech in ways that favor some viewpoints or ideas at the expense of others."[52] The *Lamb's Chapel* decision reinforces the rights of religious persons to express their views publicly.

Q Can members of the community or organizations use school facilities for religious purposes?

A Yes! Members of the local community also have free speech rights in the school if the district rents school facilities to outsiders during non-school hours. In other words, if the school district rents its facilities to non-school groups during non-school hours, then the school district has a constitutional duty to rent to religious speakers, such as a local church that wants to rent a facility for its annual Christmas pageant.[51]

The Supreme Court recently rejected an exclusion of religious

Q Can Christmas vacation still be called Christmas vacation?

A Yes! Finally, school districts are under no constitutional obligation to rename "Christmas vacation" as "Winter vacation" or some similar name. Any suggestion to the contrary is simply unnecessary and should be avoided. The Supreme Court itself has acknowledged with approval that Congress gives federal employees a paid holiday on December 25 and that Congress calls it, "Christmas."[53]

** While parents may have little direct say about what ends up in public school curricula, federal law has given parents clear rights to exempt their children from experimental or value-related classes that depart from academics. **

Opting Out Of Objectionable Classes

We live in a society where the state mandates that children attend school. Most American students attend public schools. Public schools teach a curriculum that has been required by the State Board of Education and the local school board.

Educational theories change from time to time. When those changes occur, there is a period of time when school officials try out new ideas in an attempt to find the best way to convey the knowledge to the students. One of the problems with this concept is that experimental ideas are often on the edge of what is acceptable to society. When they are implemented, parents often find their children being taught ideas that are objectionable to family beliefs.

In the past, parents had very few options when their children faced instruction from school officials that was out of step with what the family believed. Many of the families affected by this particular problem were religious, often Christian.

While parents may have little direct say about what ends up in public school curricula, federal law has given parents clear rights to exempt their children from experimental or values-related classes that depart from academics. The Hatch Amendment (passed in 1984) was designed to reinforce parental control of their children's education. Based on the Hatch Amendment, parents may have their child excluded from experimental programs.

The Hatch Amendment, also known as the Pupil Rights Amendment, says parents have the right to inspect all instructional material, including that used in experimental or testing programs. Unless parental consent is given, no student shall be required to submit to any kind of test designed to reveal information concerning political affiliations, potentially embarrassing psychological problems, sexual behavior and attitudes, illegal and anti-social behavior, critical appraisals of family relationships, legally privileged relationships (such as those with a minister or doctor), and income.

If your school introduces practices that appear related to the

occult, such as visualizing conversations with dead historical figures, chanting a mantra-like slogan, practicing any form of meditation, and so on, then the Establishment Clause of the First Amendment works on your side. The Establishment Clause forbids the state from setting up one religion over and against other religions. Since these practices are religious and state-sponsored, they represent a violation of your rights.

If you even suspect your child may be facing situations like these, attempt to find out immediately what is happening. Do not wait for your child to come home with horror stories halfway through the school year with much of the damage already done. Any sex education course or anything that appears to be remotely experimental in your child's curriculum needs thorough investigation right away. Check the materials. Meet the teacher. Question your children from day one. Whenever possible personally monitor the classes so you know week-in-and-week-out what your child is being taught.

Furthermore, stay in constant touch with your children about the content and teaching methods of what appear to be routine classes. A

> **❝ Do not wait for your child to come home with horror stories halfway through the school year with much of the damage already done.❞**

teacher can insert an unorthodox bias — whether it is amoral, anti-Christian, anti-family, anti-life, or anti-American — into any class in a potent way. Be sensitive to this possibility by staying in close contact with your child, the school and your child's teachers.

If your school system is beginning to introduce a sex education course, get involved. Lobby the school board or its designated committee to consider a traditional sex curriculum, such as Teen-Aid or Project Respect.[54] Any proper sex education course should teach abstinence as the primary and normal method of birth control prior to marriage. You will have to fight the charge that such an approach is unrealistic among today's licentious teenagers. Do not give in to such defeatist logic.

If your school system already integrates liberal sex educators such as Planned Parenthood or homosexual advocates such as California's Project 10, you probably have grounds to object. Such programs usually cross over from objective teaching to advocating amorality. Appeal to your school board that the course undermines parental authority by implying to students that everyone their age is having sex, or by teach-

ing that homosexuality is normal, or by telling students that they can easily and confidentially arrange abortions without their parents' knowledge. A religion can be any set of beliefs by which a person lives and trains their children to live, even amorality. If necessary, object on First Amendment grounds. Show that the state is illegally establishing a religion by advocating amorality.

As a more immediate tactic, find out when the outside sex program representative will be speaking to classes. Get concerned parents to take turns sitting in on classroom discussions. Planned Parenthood has been known to tidy up its presentations when parents are present.

You should try to resolve any such objectionable classroom practices locally. Appeal to the teacher, then the principal, then the school board. If those appeals fail, and you are dealing with a clear example of a school trying to implement a New Age practice, legal action could prove successful on a First Amendment basis. If appeals fail regarding values clarification or any sort of classroom therapy, the Hatch Amendment provides grounds for appeal through the U.S. Department of Education. Remember, this law does not prohibit the course, but it does prohibit your child from being included without your permission.

You can formally request that the school inform you of questionable educational materials and practices. The sample Hatch Amendment letter that follows this article can be used to make that request.

Do not be intimidated by the objection that a certain course falls outside the law because it was not developed with federal funds. The burden of proof is on the school to prove that the course used absolutely no tax money in its development, and this is unlikely. Any complaints you make should state all details of the violation. They can be filed through the Family Educational Rights and Privacy Act Office, U.S. Department of Education, 400 Maryland Ave. S.W., Washington, D.C. 20202.

Sample Hatch Amendment Letter

(Parents' Name)
(Address)
(City/State/Zip Code)

Dear _____:

I am the parent of _____ who attends _____
_____ school. Under U.S. legislation and federal court decisions, parents have the primary responsibility for their children's education, and pupils have certain rights which the school may not deny.

Parents have the right to be assured their children's beliefs and moral values are not undermined by the schools. Pupils have the right to have and to hold their values and moral standards without direct or indirect manipulations by the schools through the curricula, textbooks, audio-visual materials or supplementary assignments.

Under the Hatch Amendment, I hereby request that my child NOT be involved in any school activities or materials listed unless I have first reviewed all the relevant materials and have given my written consent for their use:

Psychological and psychiatric treatment that is designed to affect behavioral, emotional, or attitudinal characteristics of an individual or designed to elicit information about attitudes, habits, traits, opinions, beliefs or feelings of an individual or group;

Values clarifications, use of moral dilemmas, discussion of religious or moral standards, role-playing or open-ended discussions of situations involving moral issues, and survival games including life/death decision exercises;

Contrived incidents for self-revelation; sensitivity training, group-encounter sessions, talk-ins, magic-circle techniques, self-evaluation and auto-criticism; strategies designed for self-disclosure including the keeping of a diary or a journal or a log book;

Sociograms, sociodrama; psychodrama; blindfold walks; isolation techniques;

Death education, including abortion, euthanasia, suicide, use of violence, and discussions of death and dying;

Curricula pertaining to drugs and alcohol;

Nuclear war, nuclear policy and nuclear classroom games;

Globalism, one-world government or anti-nationalistic curricula;

Discussion and testing on interpersonal relationships; discussions of attitudes toward parents and parenting;

Educating in human sexuality, including pre-marital sex, contraception, abortion, homosexuality, group sex and marriages, prostitution, incest, bestiality, masturbation, divorce, population control, and roles of males and females; sex behavior and attitudes of student and family;

Pornography and any materials containing profanity and/or sexual explicitness;

Guided-fantasy techniques; hypnotic techniques; imagery and suggestology;

Organic evolution, including Darwin's theory;

Discussions of witchcraft, occultism, the supernatural, and mysticism;

Political and/or religious affiliations of students or family;

Income of family;

Non-academic personality tests; questionnaires or personal and family life attitudes.

The purpose of this letter is to preserve my child's rights under the Protection of Pupil Rights Amendment (The Hatch Amendment) to the General Education Provisions Act, and under its regulations as published in the Federal Register of September 6, 1984, which became effective November 12, 1984.

These regulations provide a procedure for filing complaints first at the local level, and then with the U.S. Department of Education. If a voluntary remedy fails, federal funds can be withdrawn from those in violation of the law.

I respectfully ask you to send me a substantive response to this letter attaching a copy of your policy statement on procedures for parental permission requirements, to notify all my child's teachers, and to keep a copy of this letter in my child's permanent file.

Thank you for your cooperation.[55]

Many people are not sure what constitutes religious discrimination in the workplace. There are many ways to discriminate against people; some are very obvious and others are more subtle. The subtle discriminations are often hard to recognize and harder still to prove in a religious discrimination claim. Therefore, we will look primarily at more outward forms of religious discrimination.

Religious discrimination includes, but is not limited to, the following: firing an employee because of that employees' Christian beliefs; loss of promotion due to one's Christian witness at work; failure to give an employee a raise until the employee no longer spends free time (such as breaks or lunch) discussing religious beliefs with other employees; harassment of employees because they wear religious clothing, such as a Christian shirt or a cross around the neck; continual mocking of a person's religious convictions or intentionally using offensive language around someone in order to mock one's religious beliefs.

Like sexual discrimination, reli-

IN THE WORKPLACE:
Fighting Religious Discrimination

"It is against the law in this country for a person to be refused a promotion or a raise or be fired due to his religious beliefs."

What Is Religious Discrimination?

will be persecuted, we should also understand that it is against the law in this country for a person to be refused a promotion or a raise or be fired due to his religious beliefs.

Many Christians are not aware they may have a religious discrimination claim against their employer if they have been harassed or fired due to their religious convictions. The Equal Employment Opportunity Commission (EEOC) is the government agency in charge of investigating claims of racial, sexual, or religious discrimination in the work place. Most Americans were probably not aware that the EEOC existed until the Clarence Thomas confirmation hearings. As you will recall, Justice Thomas was the head of the EEOC at one time.

gious discrimination is often hard to describe and harder still to define. This makes it complicated to prove that religious discrimination has occurred. Therefore, I recommend you carefully document any religious discrimination in preparation for a claim against an employer. While we as Christians are warned that those who desire to live godly lives

> **44 Many states have few laws protecting your right to work in a discrimination-free environment, thus the EEOC is often your only real remedy if you have been denied a promotion or fired because of your religious beliefs.99**

Filing A Complaint With The EEOC

Filing a complaint with the EEOC can be an effective way to resolve a legitimate religious discrimination claim. Many states have few laws protecting your right to work in a discrimination-free environment; thus the EEOC is often your only real remedy if you have been denied a promotion or fired because of your religious beliefs.

The EEOC polices the workplace by enforcing Title VII of the Civil Rights Act of 1964. Title VII prohibits discrimination based on race, color, sex, religion, or national origin. In order to make a legitimate discrimination claim under Title VII, several steps must be rigidly followed. If any of these steps is not completed within the time frame established by the government, the claim will be dismissed. These steps are time consuming and will require that you wait patiently for the EEOC to evaluate and investigate your claim.

The process for filing a complaint is very tedious. To begin the process, you must file a claim with either the state or the federal branch of the EEOC. If this step is not followed, you cannot file a federal lawsuit in a federal district court. In a state where there is an anti-discrimination law and a state agency authorized to act on your behalf, you must file a complaint with the EEOC within 300 days of the discriminatory act. If you file with the state EEOC first, you may request a review of their decision to the federal EEOC within 60 days. If there is no state agency with the authority to handle this cause of action, you must file a complaint with the EEOC within 100 days of the discriminatory act. Part of the theory behind the short time period for filing is that constitutional rights violations are so grievous that legitimate complaints will be made quickly. Furthermore, the longer you wait to file a complaint about a discriminatory act, the harder that act becomes to prove. As more and more time passes, witnesses are harder to locate, witnesses' memories get blurry, or they may lose their motivation to testify against an employer because they have been promoted.

At this point, the EEOC will

investigate your complaint to determine the validity of the claim. The investigation involves several steps. First, the EEOC will notify your employer or former employer concerning the charges you have made against him or her. Then the EEOC will request information about the charges from the employer. Witnesses who have knowledge of the discriminatory act will be interviewed. If this investigation shows there are reasonable grounds to believe a discriminatory act has occurred, the EEOC will notify you and your employer or former employer.

The EEOC will attempt to persuade your employer or former employer to eliminate voluntarily the discrimination and correct any actions that have been carried out in violation of Title VII. One remedy could include reinstating you to the position you had or would have had but for the discrimination. You could also receive lost wages and have lost benefits, such as vacation or even retirement, restored to you.

If the EEOC finds reasonable cause to believe that your complaint is actionable and all efforts at reconciliation have proven fruitless, the EEOC may file a lawsuit against

> 66 When Paul stood before the rulers in Jerusalem, he demanded his rights as a Roman citizen. When we enter a courtroom or petition the EEOC, we are responding like the apostle Paul. 99

the offending party. Within 90 days of receiving a notice of the "right-to-sue" from the EEOC, you must file a private lawsuit or you will lose your right to file a legal claim. It is important for you to know that you must request the "right-to-sue" letter from the EEOC; they will not send it automatically.

Obviously, the EEOC may conclude their investigation by determining that you do not have a reasonable ground to file a complaint against your employer or former employer. If this occurs, you do not have the right to bring a claim against your employer or former employer for religious discrimination.

If you have followed all of these steps, the 1991 Civil Rights Act allows you to request a jury trial and sue for compensatory and punitive damages. Compensatory damages cover the actual losses you have incurred as a result of the discriminatory act. Punitive damages are sought strictly to punish wrongdoers for their discriminatory act as a way of encouraging them not to discriminate in the future. To obtain the correct forms for filing a complaint with the EEOC, you should call 1-800-USA-EEOC.

This is so important that I want

to repeat it one more time. Religious discrimination claims are very serious matters. It is not enough to merely believe you have been discriminated against. Because the charge is so serious, you will be required to prove your claim. So be sure to document any discriminatory acts that are committed against you in the workplace. Also, you will find it helpful if you have other witnesses who heard or saw the discriminatory act around which your complaint revolves. If that is not possible, you should attempt to find witnesses who have experienced the same type of discrimination you have alleged in your complaint.

Title VII of the Civil Rights Act was designed to protect you in the workplace. You should not hesitate to contact the EEOC if you can show that the discriminatory act about which you are complaining actually occurred. Also remember, this type of action takes a lot of time to work through. You will need to be patient while your complaint is processed and resolved.

Unfortunately, religious discrimination is becoming more prevalent in our society. It amazes me to watch a society that claims to believe in total diversity discriminating against Christians in every arena. Often I meet Christians who

have lost their jobs or not been promoted or had their speech censored for the sole reason that they were Christians. We are the salt of the earth. Our lives are a daily reminder to the people around us that there is a God and He cares for all of us. That alone is reason enough to remain in the workplace and not sit back and allow our jobs and our voice to be taken away from us.

As the days grow darker, we must stand in the face of adversity and show forth the glory and mercy of our God. He has set us in this place, at this time, that we might win some to His kingdom. When the government has set up an agency such as the EEOC to protect our rights, we should utilize that tool to benefit the Gospel. For the same reason we go into the courtroom and ask a judge to grant us the rights we have been guaranteed under the United States Constitution, we must go to the EEOC and ask them to protect us against discrimination when it occurs. When Paul stood before the rulers in Jerusalem, he demanded his rights as a Roman citizen; he demanded to be brought before Caesar. When we enter a courtroom or petition the EEOC, we are responding like the apostle Paul.

Here I want to explore ways to protect First Amendment freedoms without resorting to the courtroom. Issues brought before public local government meetings are often best dealt with by an attorney. Addressing school board or city council meetings may require an in-depth knowledge of the law and how it works. It may even require the same preparation as an attorney puts into developing a court case. The American Center for Law and Justice has vast experience handling school boards and city councils. We have sent attorneys to these meetings around the country. By using the strategies that follow, we have been able to resolve serious problems successfully without ever going to court.

Local school boards and city councils are appropriate bodies for hearing concerns on a wide variety of issues. For example, school boards consider issues involving school curricula, school facility access (for example, whether they must allow religious groups to use school facilities after school hours), and students' rights on campus. Students' rights on campus include the right to distribute literature, the

MAKING A DIFFERENCE: Changing Local Laws

66When a school board or city council has wrongfully denied someone the right to proclaim the Gospel, a channel for preaching and evangelism is lost.99

A Strategy Session

right to initiate and participate in a Bible club during the school day, the right to pray with friends during the day or before school starts, the right to wear Christian T-shirts, the right to bring a Bible to school and read it during free time, the right to pray at graduation ceremonies, the right to make a speech giving God glory during graduation, and the right to hold a baccalaureate service during the graduation season. Each of these issues are appropriate for going before the school board and voicing an opinion on what the school board must do to secure students' constitutional rights.

City councils and other local government bodies also have a wide range of issues with which they are concerned. Some of these are: evangelism in public places, such as city streets, sidewalks and local public parks; concerts in public parks; rallies or Christian crusades in public facilities, such as the city auditorium or civic center; the right to distribute literature in public places, such as streets, sidewalks and public parks; pornography ordinances; and zoning ordinances involving churches and parade ordinances for marches on public streets. You can go before your city council and express your opinion on what the city council must do to secure local citizens' or churches' constitutional rights in these areas and others.

While I recommend that attorneys make the presentations to local school boards and city councils, I wrote this section to educate people who have no legal training so they could walk into a board or council meeting and comfortably present an issue and request the board or council to resolve the problem.

If you happen to be an attorney, it is important for you to approach your presentation before a school board or city council the same way you would approach a presentation before a court. These civic bodies are filled with professionals who appreciate a well thought-out, thorough, concise presentation. You cannot be too prepared.

If you are not an attorney, the principles found in this section will still help you prepare for a school board or city council meeting.

The law is clear: First Amendment freedoms must be protected. However, it is important how the law concerning these freedoms is

> **❝ Student free speech is most often blocked by *local* regulations, not state regulations. City parks and sidewalks are most often shut down by *local* city commissions rather than by state regulations. ❞**

presented to local school boards and city councils. The responsibility of representing First Amendment issues before school boards and city councils requires a spokesperson who is able to utilize a wide range of skills, including abilities in legal research, negotiation, communications and public relations. This type of representation demands not only proficiency in a variety of procedures, but also a mindfulness of sensitive local issues since the community is so directly involved.

Preliminary evaluation is essential to a successful presentation. You must closely examine the facts. Then these facts must be applied to the legal precedents in your area and the Supreme Court. If you fail to properly evaluate your case, the entire presentation could be off-base and ineffective. Once you evaluate these components, you must weigh them in the context of the theory and nature of the result desired. For example, your presentation might be before a local city council who has forbidden the distribution of literature on city streets because of the littering problem. Rather than spend the entire meeting on the right to distribute literature under the First Amendment, you could simply point out that the Supreme Court has held that littering ordinances are invalid when they are used to stop otherwise protected free speech.

The sense of community goodwill you bring to your case and presentation cannot be over emphasized. Local leaders, including school officials, school board members, city council members, attorneys, and the media need to understand that you support them while attempting to resolve the issues in question. It is in the best interest of all parties if you can diffuse potentially explosive situations early in the process.

In addition to these matters, it is very important that you factor in the very nature of the action itself. A contention over the free speech attributes of the distribution of literature might not awaken the general population. But the recent issues revolving around graduation prayer could stimulate the entire community, including both school board officials and their attorneys on the local and state level. A case involving equal access to public facilities can serve as a rallying point for the Christian community in garnering local support. In all these situations, the spokesperson

> **66 The sense of community goodwill you bring to your case and presentation cannot be over emphasized. Try to diffuse potentially explosive situations early in the process. 99**

plays a key role in assuring that all parties maintain the proper perspective and that you understand the implications involved.

At the heart of any dispute or discussion with school boards or city councils is the particular strategy chosen to resolve the problem successfully. Even though attorneys are trained to evaluate and litigate, there are times when the concern about litigation from a social and/or biblical perspective closes the door to litigation, thereby making an out-of-court settlement the only way to resolve the dispute. Out-of-court settlements can help to establish good rapport with local officials, which can lead to alliance building that can be quite useful in future situations.

With the emergence of new rulings on these and related issues, it is absolutely necessary that a presenter engage in accurate research and interpretation of case law. While this may be overlooked, failure to accurately identify legal issues relevant to the case and then apply the necessary legal authority can easily result in disaster.

On the other hand, attention to the details of defending clients before school boards and city councils can yield more than a successful resolution — it can foster long-term working relationships within the community which can foster a more accepting environment for the exercise of First Amendment freedoms.

> **"Our goal is to keep open all channels of communication so our message can be heard in the public arena, not just in our homes and churches."**

Practical Tips For Making Your Case

Q Why should I consider the strategy of working through the local government group that decides who is allowed access to property under its control?

A Our job as Christians is to share the Gospel and confront contemporary issues from a biblical perspective. At the American Center, our goal is to keep open all channels of communication so our message can be heard in the public arena, not just in our homes and churches. When a school board or

city council has wrongfully denied someone the right to proclaim the Gospel, a channel for preaching and evangelism is lost. We want to re-open that channel as quickly as possible.

Q Why are local boards and councils a good place to change policies in the community?

A Local government bodies are the first line of decision-making. Local schools are primarily run by local school boards, not courts or state school boards. Student free speech is most often blocked by *local* regulations, not state regulations. City parks and sidewalks are most often shut down by *local* city commissions rather than by state regulations.

Local board and council members are usually elected. Elected officials are very sensitive to the fact that an unhappy public is not the best way to get reelected. Most public officials desire to be reelected. When the coverage they receive is negative, board or council members want to change that image. That means they are more likely to get on the side of parents and other citizens who can rally support for a local board meeting. Why? Because these same people can also rally votes during election time. Politicians need vote-getters, not just voters, so their ears perk up when support looms large for a cause they may have not championed in the past.

Additionally, boards and councils make policies that affect the local communities they govern. While Washington, D.C., is far away, the local courthouse or boardroom is just around the corner. The local board's influence is more readily felt by the community, hence it is a good place to start when changing local policies.

Moreover, by working through a local board, two potential problems are avoided. First, there is the problem of time. The board has often made a wrong decision based on misinformation. They wrongly believe they have the authority to discriminate against Christian speech because of the so-called "separation of church and state." If the local board can be educated, the problem can be resolved within days rather than the months, even years, it could take to work the matter through the courts. Therefore, to save valuable time and energy, not to mention financial resources, the best strategy is often to go straight to the local board to resolve the problem.

The other problem is community relations. By educating the board, a local Christian church or group can resolve the misunderstanding that has created the problem without offending the community in the process. The public does not have an

> **❝ Local officials do not relish court battles any more than anyone else. If you can help them avoid one, they may rise up and call you blessed. ❞**

accurate concept of the legal process and, therefore, they often view all litigation as hostile. So while a court battle may be won, the community relations war will have been lost. This does not mean a matter should never be litigated. If negotiations fail or education proves impossible, the option of a legal remedy in the courtroom still exists. Nevertheless, whenever possible, resolving the case through the local boards is the better approach. In fact, especially in tight economic times, what local government group would sacrifice the opportunity to save taxpayers' money while upholding the Constitution just to win a court case? Local officials do not relish court battles any more than anyone else. If you can help them avoid one, they may rise up and call you blessed.

Q How do I get on the agenda?

A Usually agendas are set one to several months in advance. Therefore, preplanning must begin early enough to allow the political machinery time to function. If a person approaches the board on a Monday just before a Tuesday board meeting, the chairman of the board may or may not allow her to appear on the agenda and address the board. If that same person had requested at a much earlier time that she be placed on the agenda it would have been no problem.

If you are from out of town, you might want to have the client or some other local person get your name on the agenda. But be sure to follow up on your request. Sometimes the local person may be convinced that the board or council is putting you on the agenda, but he has not checked to ensure that this is the case. Never assume you are on the agenda. A quick phone call will determine if the proper steps have been followed and you are on board to speak. Our attorneys always place a follow-up phone call to ensure they are on the board or council meeting agenda. This helps avoid unnecessary expense and undue embarrassment.

Q How do I build community support before the board meeting?

A Work with your local churches. When a local church sees the need for involvement, they will sound the cry for help. A pastor is in a good position to explain the need to his congregation once he knows what the need is.

Many communities have groups in place that are involved in local political issues. These groups have the contacts needed to alert the community. They usually have close relationships with at least one or two local churches. Therefore, local community action groups can be very helpful in building community support that will help affect changes in your area.

Q How do I lay the proper groundwork for the maximum effect in the community?

A In addition to appealing to local churches, there are several other ways to lay the proper groundwork for the maximum effect in your community. Most communities have para-church organizations that are willing to help heighten community awareness. Because these organizations work with different churches rather than within any one church, they are better able to spread the word to more members of the community. One of the roles of a para-church ministry is to develop contacts in and around the community. These contacts can be helpful in a campaign designed to stimulate community awareness.

Local and national civic groups are another way of involving the local community. These groups constantly look for worthy projects to sponsor. Like a para-church ministry, civic groups draw people from a variety of lifestyles which serves to heighten community awareness.

It is important to have the people who are affected by the board or council decision at the meeting. If the school board is voting on an issue that affects students in the community, it is helpful to have students present. Often we request that students be allowed to address the school board as well as our attorney. This assures that the school board realizes that the vote they are about to take affects real lives. We ask parents to come as well. By their presence, parents send a two-fold message: they are concerned about the decisions that affect their children; they are voters and this meeting might well determine how they vote. This approach is not manipulation; it is the American political process at work.

The same approach should be taken with a city council. Whoever will be affected by the council vote should be present at the meeting. We often request time for them to address the council members for the same reason we ask students to address a school board.

Every person present at a board or council meeting represents a percentage of the community. By attending a meeting we let elected officials know we are watching how they vote. This monitoring devise was built into our system by our founding fathers. It reminds our political leaders that if they do not do what the people want, the people have the right to elect someone else. Our political system works best when people are involved in the

> **66** Every person present at a board or council meeting represents a percentage of the community. By attending a meeting we let elected officials know we are watching how they vote. **99**

process. Apathy destroys the system; participation improves it.

Q Should I involve the press?

A We seldom speak to the press before we go into court. Board and council presentations, however, present a different situation. Boards and councils are political bodies and therefore, by definition, more subject to community pressure than a court — and rightly so. The press can make a poorly-attended board or council meeting a hot item in the community. Suddenly, the school board or city council is looking at several hundred parents or citizens who expect to get a satisfactory answer from them at that meeting. Each of these parents or citizens translates into a person who is concerned enough to take the time to attend a meeting. If they are that concerned, they are most likely concerned enough to vote and influence others to vote too.

The press can alert the community to a need of which they may have been unaware. Many Christians view the press as an enemy, and never stop to realize that the local press often merely presents local community happenings. Christians should learn to alert the press about particular events. We should be willing to use the press to alert the community of the decisions of local political leaders, such as school boards or city council members. Publicity often brings accountability to local political bodies.

(For more information on this topic, see Appendix II on dealing with the media.)

> 66 **When you come before the board with a prepared text, the facts will be clear in your head, the law will be on the tip of your tongue, and you will speak with greater eloquence and clarity.** 99

Q When I am appearing before a board, should I use a written presentation or speak entirely extemporaneously?

A It is important to be prepared when speaking to boards or councils. The benefit of preparing a written statement is that it forces focus. When speaking at meetings such as a school board or a city council, time is usually very limited. Members of those bodies work full-time jobs and appreciate brevity. Lengthy addresses tend to distract from your role as counselor and concerned citizen. They can also create confusion rather than resolve it, since longer talks tend to ramble.

When you come before the board with a prepared text, the facts will be clear in your head, the law will be on the tip of your tongue, and you will speak with greater eloquence and clarity. That will cause you to stand out before the board and give greater credibility to your comments.

This does not mean, though, that you should be inflexible. After all, situations can change and cause your speech to be outdated. For example, one of our attorneys was speaking to a park commission in Boston, Massachusetts. He had prepared a statement for the commissioners in anticipation of their meeting. All prior indications led to the conclusion that the commission would not attempt to censor the religious speech of a local pastor in their park, so our attorney's prepared speech was very conciliatory. As the meeting began, however, it became obvious that even though the board would agree to allow the pastor to speak in the park, board members were unhappy that they were being "forced" to allow the speech to occur uncensored. Hence, our attorney's prepared talk had to be adapted to fit the unexpected situation. If he had delivered it as originally written, it would have missed the point. Was it therefore a wasted effort? Not at all. The prepared speech allowed our attorney to be knowledgeable enough about the situation to effectively and forcefully adapt his presentation to fit the need of the moment.

Q How do I make my oral presentation to the board?

A Any time you address a board or council you must remember to be animated and forceful without being obnoxious or arrogant. Let the tone of your presentation reflect the mood of the board or council. If the board is working to resolve the problem, you should be forceful yet friendly. If the board is dragging their feet, you should be forceful and insistent. If the board is refusing to protect your or your client's First Amendment freedoms, you should be forceful and aggressive. Remember, boards and councils are political bodies; they will respond to community pressure. A well-argued, powerful presentation may well influence them to protect First Amendment freedoms.

Also, boards and councils see a host of presentations during the course of a year. Their time is limited and they have many things on their minds when you are there. So grab their attention by being knowledgeable. Do not force them to guess what you want — tell them straight out. And in the process, lay out the facts and the law in the same way you would to a court, while being

> ** 66 Our political system works best when people are involved in the process. Apathy destroys the system; participation improves it. 99**

conscious of the fact that your audience is not likely composed of lawyers. Remember, board or council members are not as aware of the situation as you are, especially the situation as viewed through your client's eyes. So make sure your presentation fosters clarity and understanding at every turn. Board and council members are not mindreaders; they must be told what is expected of them by you and the Constitution and why.

Q Once I have spoken to the board or council, is my job through?

A No. Follow-up is probably the most important job you have when you are working with a local school board or city council. These boards and councils are administrative bodies, and often an idea gets lost or confused on the way from the meeting to the application of the idea. The process of reaching a decision is filled with give and take. Confusion often develops during the course of a meeting as to what the board or council members are merely discussing, and what the board or council has actually decided. After a decision has been reached, the decision will often be written out for clarity's sake. While the board or council may sincerely intend for the idea to be implemented the way it was discussed during the meeting, the clerk, or whoever types up the decision, may not convey what the board intended. Additionally, whenever communication takes place, there is always the potential for misunderstanding. Because people approach conversations and negotiations from different vantage points, they may leave a discussion thinking that the other side is happy — only to discover that when the terms of the agreement are finally reduced to writing, the written statement does not represent what each side thought they had agreed to. Therefore, you should always follow up a presentation or negotiation.

Follow-up is simple. A phone call or letter is usually adequate to confirm that everything is moving ahead properly. At the American Center, we always follow up our presentations with a letter. Usually we request a copy of any decisions or rules that came from the meeting. It also allows us to look over what the board or council agreed to and evaluate the new guidelines in light of what is legal and what best serves the interests of our client.

Q **What result has the American Center seen from addressing**

the problem at the board and council meeting level rather than in the courtroom?

A The results have been extremely favorable. When we attend board and council meetings, we are there on behalf of members of the local community. We are there with a full knowledge of the constitutional principles involved. We are there to help resolve the problem. We do not approach the board or council with haughtiness, yet we are prepared to stand up for the rights of Christians. To this point, we have never been to a board or council meeting where we were unable to work out a solution that was acceptable to the people we represented.

Our government was originally designed to work according to the desires of the people. Government must be responsive to the voice of the governed if it is to be effective. When you attend a board or council meeting and speak up, your voice is heard. Local government bodies are very responsive to the voice of the governed, even though that is less often the case with national government bodies. Local board and council members realize they have to look local citizens in the eye after they make their decisions. Your presence and voice at a local board or council meeting can make a difference, but you must be prepared.

Students are vested with two distinct sets of rights in the public school setting. First, all students retain their constitutionally protected right to freedom of speech and expression. Second, the federal Equal Access Act guarantees high school students the right to have Bible clubs on campus.

The Supreme Court has addressed the right of students to express their opinions on their public school campuses. Specifically, the Court has held that students and teachers do not "shed their constitutional rights...at the schoolhouse gate."[56] This principle means that students rightfully on a public school campus have First Amendment rights that cannot be denied without reason. It is important to note that the 8th Circuit in *Mergens* held that students have a First Amendment right and an Equal Access Act right to hold a student-initiated Bible club meeting on campus.[57] Thus, even in the event that a school has not allowed any noncurriculum clubs to meet, the *Tinker* rule would still require that students be allowed to associate with other stu-

"Students rightfully on a public school campus have First Amendment rights that cannot be denied without reason."

The Federal Constitution

dents in Bible clubs. School officials must be very careful about abridging the rights of students who are rightfully on campus.

Material or Substantial Disruption: The Heart of *Tinker*

Under the *Tinker* decision, a principal cannot prohibit student speech simply because he believes there will be a disruption of the educational process. In fact, he can only restrict student speech if it will "materially or substantially disrupt school discipline."[58] Students have the right to discuss religious beliefs, and even share religious materials, with their peers between classes, at break, at lunch, and before and after school. As the Court declared:

> *It can hardly be argued that either students or teachers shed their constitutional rights to freedom of speech or expression at the schoolhouse gate. This has been the unmistakable holding of this Court for almost 50 years.*[59]

In the nearly 25 years since *Tinker*, the Supreme Court has continued this holding. It has now been the Court's holding for almost 75 years.

Tinker's holding did not depend on a finding that the school was a public forum. The Court emphasized, instead, that "[w]hen [a student] is in the cafeteria, or on the playing field, or on the campus during the authorized hours, he may express his opinions...."[60] Therefore, whether or not a school campus constitutes a public forum for non-students, it is clear that the students who are required to attend have the protection of First Amendment Free Speech guarantees.

Fundamental Rights of Students

Our educational system requires students to attend schools. This coercion gives students the legal right to be on campus. As Justice Fortas noted:

> In our system, state-operated schools may not be enclaves of totalitarianism. School officials do not possess absolute authority over their students. Students in school as well as out of school are 'persons' under our Constitution. They are possessed of fundamental rights which the State must respect, just as they themselves must respect their obligations to the

State. In our system, students may not be regarded as closed-circuit recipients of only that which the State chooses to communicate. They may not be confined to the expression of those sentiments that are officially approved. In the absence of a specific showing of constitutionally valid reasons to regulate their speech, students are entitled to freedom of expression of their views. As Judge Gewin, speaking for the Fifth Circuit, said, school officials cannot suppress "expressions of feelings with which they do not wish to contend."[61]

Student Rights On Campus After *Tinker*

After *Tinker*, the law regarding the First Amendment rights of students is well-established. Student speech cannot be restricted because of the content of that speech. School administrators can only prohibit protected speech by students when it "materially and substantially interfere[s] with the requirements of appropriate discipline in the operation of the school."[62]

It is well settled that religious speech is protected by the First Amendment of the Constitution, even when that speech is taking place on the public school campus.[63] In fact, the right to persuade, advocate or evangelize a religious viewpoint, implicates the very reason the First Amendment was adopted. As the Supreme Court held in *Thomas v. Collins*:

> [T]he protection [the Framers] saw was not solely for persons in intellectual pursuits. It extends to more than abstract discussion unrelated to action. The First Amendment is a charter for government, not for an institution of learning. **Free trade in ideas** means free trade and the opportunity to persuade, not merely to describe facts.[64]

The nature of public schools does not justify the forfeiture of Constitutional rights. In fact, the public nature of such schools enhances the Constitutional rights of students. The school is the best place to teach students how the laws of the land apply.

The Equal Access Act

The Supreme Court held, in *Widmar v. Vinvent*, that when colleges allowed student groups to use their facilities they could not discriminate against student religious groups.[65] In other words, Christian students have to be allowed to use a meeting room on campus with the same restrictions applied to any other student group. The Establishment Clause of the First Amendment is not violated when a government entity, such as a public university, treats all groups the same, without attempting to censor religious speech. The *Mergens* Court quoted from *Widmar* extensively as they explained why secondary students have the right to have religious clubs on their campus.

Congress enacted the Equal Access Act to cure pervasive anti-religious bigotry exhibited by public secondary school officials in the aftermath of the Supreme Court's school prayer cases. Three factors determine whether the Equal Access Act compels official recognition of a Bible club by school officials: 1) does the school receive federal funds; 2) is the school a public secondary school; and 3) does the school allow any noncurriculum clubs to meet on campus?

When these factors are satisfied, federal law compels school officials to provide equal access to students who want to organize and conduct Bible clubs and student prayer groups.

In *Garnett v. Renton School Dist. No. 403*, a Federal Court of Appeals ruled that the Equal Access Act must be complied with even in the face of a state constitutional provision to the contrary.[66]

WESTSIDE COMMUNITY SCHOOLS V. MERGENS

The United States Supreme Court upheld the constitutionality of the Equal Access Act in *Westside Community Schools v. Mergens (Mergens)*.[67] According to the *Mergens* Court, the above-mentioned factors should be employed in a standard three-prong analysis, as follows:

1. Federal Funding. Does the school receive any federal funds at all? This question is answered, simply, yes or no. If the answer is no, the Equal Access Act does not apply. If the answer is yes, it is necessary to examine the next prong of the *Mergens*-Equal Access Act test.

2. Secondary Schools. Is the school in question a secondary school as defined by state law? This information should be available from the local State Board of Education. If the school in question is classified as a secondary school, it is then necessary to examine the third prong of the *Mergens*-Equal Access Act test. While it varies from state to state, most states classify a secondary school as grades nine through twelve.

3. Noncurriculum Clubs on Campus. Does the school allow noncurriculum clubs to meet on campus? Here the *Mergens* Court was very specific. Schools cannot misrepresent the nature of clubs that are permitted to meet. The Court explicitly examined the intent of Congress concerning noncurriculum-related clubs:

> *[W]e think that the term 'noncurriculum related student group' is best interpreted broadly to mean any student group that does not directly relate to the body of courses offered by the school. In our view, a student group directly relates to a school's curriculum if the subject matter of the group is actually taught, or will soon be taught, in a regularly offered course; if the subject matter of the group concerns the body of courses as a whole; if participation in the group is required for a particular course; or if participation in the group results in academic credit....This...definition...is consistent with Congress' intent to provide a low threshold for triggering the [Equal Access] Act's requirements.*[68]

Thus, the nature of the clubs currently meeting at the school is key. Service clubs, for example, such as the Key Club, the Lions Club, Zonta and Interact are not considered curriculum-related.

Additionally, clubs such as the Chess Club do not relate to the curriculum under normal circumstances. For example, only when a school teaches chess as an academic subject, for which students received a grade, would a Chess Club be considered related to the curriculum. The school district's argument, in *Mergens*, that chess was curriculum related because it enhanced logical thinking and the performance of mathematical calculations was rejected by the Supreme Court.

In *Mergens*, Justice O'Connor noted that "if a state refused to let religious groups use the facilities open to others, then it would demonstrate not neutrality but hostility toward religion. The Establishment Clause does not license government to treat religion and those who teach or practice it, simply by virtue of their status as such, as subversive of American ideals and therefore subject to unique disabilities."[69] When a public high school official refuses to allow student-initiated Bible clubs treatment equal to that given other non-curriculum clubs meeting on campus, it treats those students as second-class citizens. This attitude is precisely the one which the Equal Access Act prohibits.

BIBLE CLUBS MUST RECEIVE OFFICIAL RECOGNITION

Official recognition means that the Bible club must be treated the same as other clubs meeting on campus. "Official recognition allows student clubs to be part of the student activities program and carries with it access to the school newspaper, bulletin boards, the public address system, and the annual Club Fair."[70] Under that view, Bible clubs are allowed to advertise on campus. Types of advertisement could include, but are not limited to: flyers distributed among other students, posters displayed on the school walls, notices in the school newspaper and announcements included during the morning or afternoon announcements. It is important to note that the Bible club is not responsible to make sure the students know that the club is student-initiated. Rather, this is a responsibility of school officials.

Once the Equal Access Act is triggered, the school must provide a room for the Bible club. The school must also make its resources available to the Bible club in the same way that those resources are made available to other clubs. Additionally, the Bible club must be allowed to meet at any time other clubs are allowed to meet. If there is a club period, the Bible club must be allowed to meet during that period.

If other clubs are allowed to have school-wide assemblies to espouse their views, then the Bible club must be allowed the same privilege. Secondary school officials are not allowed to discriminate against a student group because of its message. Neither is a secondary school official allowed to censor the speech of the Bible Club by requiring it to delete references to Christianity from the club's constitution, announcements, or other materials.

SPONSORS V. CUSTODI- ANS: FACULTY/STAFF

The only difference between a Bible club and any other club allowed to meet on the school campus is the use of faculty members as club sponsors. The Equal Access Act specifically allows for a faculty/staff custodian as compared to a normal club sponsor. This means that the faculty/staff custodian does not have control of the Bible club. He or she is only there to ensure that the Bible club does not violate school policies.

The Bible club must be student-initiated. This means that students must create and lead the club. It does not mean that they cannot have outside speakers. It only means that a non-student cannot lead the club. Community leaders and others can be invited to speak occasionally.

Literature Distribution

Students' First Amendment rights include the right to distribute Gospel tracts during non-instructional time, the right to wear shirts with overtly Christian messages and symbols, and the right to pray and discuss matters of religion with others. Further, schools may not prevent students from bringing their Bibles to school. In fact, school officials must allow students to read their Bibles during free time, even if that free time occurs during class.

The standard that must be applied by the school is: Does the activity "materially or substantially disrupt school discipline?" Unless a student is participating in activities that are disruptive, the school must allow them to continue.

As a preliminary matter, it is a constitutional axiom that the distribution of free religious literature is a form of expression protected by the First Amendment. Religious and political speech are protected by the First Amendment.[71] Furthermore, "advocacy and persuasive speech are included within the First Amendment guarantee if the speech is otherwise protected."[72]

The United States Supreme Court's consistent jurisprudence, for over 50 years, recognizes the free distribution of literature as a form of expression protected by the United States Constitution.[73] In *Lovell*, the United States Supreme Court put the case for constitutional protection of leaflets and pamphlets quite clearly:

> *The liberty of the press is not confined to newspapers and periodicals. It necessarily embraces pamphlets and leaflets. These indeed have been historic weapons in the defense of liberty, as the pamphlets of Thomas Paine and others in our history abundantly attest. The press in its historic connotation comprehends every sort of publication which affords a vehicle of*

*information and opinion.
What we have had recent
occasion to say with
respect to the vital importance of protecting this
essential liberty from every
sort of infringement need
not be repeated.*[74]

Of course, the constitutional
value of leaflets and pamphlets is
not lessened by the fact that they
address matters of religion. The
materials at issue in *Lovell* were "a
pamphlet and magazine in the
nature of religious tracts...."[75] Just
five years after *Lovell*, in *Murdock
v. Pennsylvania*, the United States
Supreme Court said:

*The hand distribution of
religious tracts is an age-
old form of missionary
evangelism — as old as
the history of printing
presses. It has been a
potent force in various religious movements down
through the years....It is
more than preaching; it is
more than distribution of
religious literature. It is a
combination of both. Its
purpose is as evangelical
as the revival meeting.
This form of religious
activity occupies the same
high estate under the First
Amendment as do worship
in the churches and preaching from the pulpits.*[76]

School officials may not lump a

student's right to distribute free
literature together with more disruptive forms of expression, such as
solicitation. In a recent decision, a
plurality of the Supreme Court
noted the experience of thousands of
"residents of metropolitan areas
[who] know from daily experience
[that] confrontation by a person
asking for money disrupts passage
and is more intrusive and intimidating than an encounter with a person
giving out information."[77] In fact,
distribution of literature is, inher-
ently, even less disruptive than
spoken expression. As the Supreme
Court stated, "[o]ne need not ponder
the contents of a leaflet or pamphlet
in order mechanically to take it out
of someone's hand, but one must
listen, comprehend, decide and act
in order to respond to a
solicitation."[78]

The applicable standard — material and substantial disruption — is
not met by an undifferentiated fear
or apprehension of disruption. In
other words, it is not enough for
school officials to fear that allowing
religious speech will offend some
members of the community. As the
Supreme Court said, "in our system,
undifferentiated fear or apprehension of disturbance is not enough to
overcome the right to freedom of
expression."[79] Where a student
wishes to peacefully distribute free
literature on school grounds during
non-instructional time, there simply
is nothing which "might reasonably
[lead] school authorities to forecast
substantial disruption or material
interference with school activities...."[80]

In fact, several courts have held that the distribution of religious literature by high school students is protected speech under the First Amendment and Fourteenth Amendment.[81] Note that in *Hemry* school officials ultimately conceded that students had the right to distribute the religious material on campus both inside and outside the school building.[82]

As the Supreme Court clearly held in *Tinker*:

> In our system, state-operated schools may not be enclaves for totalitarianism. School officials do not possess absolute authority over their students. Students in school as well as out of school are persons under our Constitution. They are possessed of fundamental rights which the state must respect, just as they themselves must respect their obligations to the state. In our system, students may not be regarded as closed-circuit recipients of only that which the state chooses to communicate. They may not be confined to the expressions of those sentiments that are officially approved.[83]

While school officials may seek to distinguish *Tinker* as inapplicable by arguing that a public school is not a traditional public forum, such assertions are unavailing because "[t]he holding in *Tinker* did not depend upon a finding that the school was a public forum."[84] As the *Tinker* Court noted, when a student "is in the cafeteria, or on the playing field, or on the campus during the authorized hours, he may express his opinions...."[85]

Further, as the *Rivera* court noted, "whether or not a school campus is available as the public forum to others, it is clear that the students, who of course are required to be in school, have the protection of the First Amendment while they are lawfully in attendance."[86] The *Tinker* Court also recognized that "personal intercommunication among students" in high schools is an activity to which schools are dedicated.[87]

Certainly, it is necessary to acknowledge that school officials have "important, delicate and highly discretionary functions" to perform.[88] These functions, however, must be performed "within the limits of the Bill of Rights."[89] "The vigilant protection of constitutional freedoms is nowhere more vital than in a community of American schools."[90]

School officials need not fear that distribution activities of students may be imputed to them, and that the Establishment Clause would thereby be violated. This very argument has been reviewed and rejected by the United States Supreme Court. In *Mergens*, the Supreme Court stated, as a general proposition, that the activities of student evangelists in a public school do not present any Establishment Clause problem:

> *Petitioner's principal contention is that the Act has the primary effect of advancing religion. Specifically, petitioners urge that, because the student religious meetings are held under school aegis, and because the state's compulsory attendance laws bring the students together (and thereby provide a ready-made audience for student evangelists), an objective observer in the position of a secondary school student will perceive official school support for such religious meetings....We disagree.*[91]

Of course, *Mergens* merely reflects the Establishment Clause's intended limitation — not on the rights of individual students — but on the power of governments (including school officials). As the *Mergens* Court stated, "there is a crucial difference between *government* speech endorsing religion, which the Establishment Clause forbids, and *private* speech endorsing religion, which the Free Speech and Free Exercise Clauses protect."[92]

KNOWING YOUR RIGHTS MEDIA GUIDE

> **66** There are at least two sides to every story. You can bet the folks on the other side of the issue will tell their story to a reporter. You should too. **99**

Q What happens when I am contacted by the news media? How do I respond?

A In many communities, news reporters routinely cover local government activities, including school board meetings. For example, if you address a school board meeting, you may find that a reporter is in the audience. This presents an excellent opportunity to share your concerns with the school board and with the news media, which ultimately means the public. There are at least two sides to every story. You can bet the folks on the other side of the issue will take advantage of an opportunity to tell their story to a reporter. You should too.

Q How do I handle such a request? What do I say to a reporter?

A The best way to handle a request from a news reporter is to be open and direct. Most reporters do not cover one topic. They bounce around, often covering a myriad of subjects in any given week. But even if they are covering a particular issue, they may still be unaware of your concerns on the issue and perhaps even ill-informed about the issue's intricacies. You can help educate the reporter, while at the same time taking advantage of an opportunity to express your side of the story. Be clear and concise. Make sure you know what you want to say and how you will say it. Get to the bottom line quickly. Focus on one or two key points. Keep it simple. Do not get bogged down with too many details. Try to explain the essence of your position in a sentence or two. Reporters work under tight time and space limitations. They often must condense a complicated issue into a few sentences or paragraphs. Why not help them by being clear and concise? When you do, you increase your chances that the news coverage will be fair, balanced, and accurate.

Q How can I guarantee that my position will not be misstated? If I do not talk to a reporter, then I cannot be misquoted, right? Isn't that the best thing to do?

A There are no guarantees concerning the outcome of a news story. Believe it or not, most reporters are not conspiring to slant a story one way or the other. Most are professionals who strive to tell both sides of a story with balance and fairness. But, of course, you cannot be sure what information will be used and what information will be withheld. You certainly cannot be sure how it will be presented. But there is one thing you can know with certainty: If you do not offer your point of view and remain silent, you will have no input in the story. You will not be misquoted, but what could even be more damaging, you will not be quoted either. To compete equally in the marketplace of ideas, you must deal with the news media. You need to get your ideas and concerns into the marketplace, and one of the best ways to do that is through the media.

Q **I do not want to be treated unfairly, though. How can I maximize the chances that my comments will be presented without bias? I just want to get a "fair shake."**

A Again, the best approach is one of openness and clarity. Tell your story in a concise manner. There is nothing wrong with asking a reporter, "Do you understand what I am trying to say?" By asking that question, you give the reporter an opportunity to tell you how they perceive your position. Remember, communication is the key. You need to be direct, honest, and concise. Do not be afraid to repeat yourself. State your position. Re-state it. Re-state it again, if necessary. As I

mentioned earlier, reporters often learn about a story as they are covering it. Help the education process along. Be ready, willing, and able to provide a reporter with any additional information (written or otherwise) to help clarify and reinforce your position. Do not overload a reporter with a ream of documents, but a well-placed supporting document or two never hurts. In most instances, you will have just one opportunity to make your point. Take advantage of it.

Q **All right, what happens if I participate and I am still misquoted? What do I do if the newspaper or TV news story is not accurate?**

The first thing you should do is stop and take a deep breath. If you feel the story was biased or unfair, you will likely be upset, angry, or worse. Calm down before you do anything. Before you take any action, ask yourself these questions: "Was the news story fair? Were both sides of the story presented and given equal treatment?" Re-read the story or play back the videotape before you answer. Notice I said both sides of the story. Sometimes we have a tendency to overreact and think a story is unfair because it includes criticism or opposition. Remember, a story is fair and balanced if it includes both sides of a story and treats both equally. A fair and balanced story should never be an advocacy piece for either side, including your own. If after considering all this, you still come to the conclusion the story was unfair, you should contact the reporter who did the story. Express your concerns in a calm fashion. No one likes to get a phone call from a screamer. Discuss the story and explain why you felt your position was misstated or treated unfairly. Use specifics. Remember, keep the lines of communication open. Do not threaten a reporter with a line like, "I will never talk to you again!" That may make you feel better, but it does not accomplish anything.

Your goal should be to develop trusting relationships with reporters and editors. That is right, I said trusting. The newspaper, radio, or television station is going to remain part of your community, and unless you decide to move away, you will no doubt deal with the media again. It will be to your advantage to get to know a reporter or a news editor. You do not have to become best buddies, but you need to talk with them, even when they are not doing a story that concerns you. By developing a relationship with them, you will get to know them better, and more importantly, they will get to know you better. This builds trust. Trust helps keep the lines of communication open. And that is an important building block to fair and balanced news coverage.

By the way, if you think a reporter has done a good job with a story, pick up the phone and tell them. They like to hear that also.

Q If I have an interesting news story or would like some coverage about a specific event, what is the best way of going about contacting a reporter?

A The more comfortable you become dealing with the news media, the more likely you will want to initiate the contact. Remember, equal access to the marketplace of ideas means learning how to deal with the news media, and that should include being pro-active. Reporters are always looking for news stories, and news stories center around ideas, issues, events, and people. You can alert reporters to potential news items and thereby become a valuable resource. So do not be afraid to initiate the contact. This is where developing a relationship with a reporter is very beneficial. If you know someone at the newspaper, radio or TV station, pick up the phone and give them a call. Let them know what is on your mind. Ask them who you should talk to about your potential story.

If you do not have a personal contact in the news department, try calling a news editor or an assignment editor. They are the decision-makers when it comes to covering a news story. Follow up the phone call with a letter or information that can be faxed to their attention. Remember, reporters have to work on tight schedules, so the faster they can get information, the better. Fax machines provide instant access. But do not abuse the opportunity.

No news organization likes to be bombarded with a proliferation of lengthy news releases. Be selective of what you send, and keep it short.

One final note: Respect deadlines. If you call a reporter or an editor and he cannot talk to you, do not be offended. Chances are he is trying to beat a deadline. Ask him when it would be convenient for you to call back. As a general rule, avoid contacting news rooms in the late afternoon or early evening. That is when most reporters and editors are under the gun (particularly in the television industry). Generally, the best time to call reporters is early morning, after they have had their first cup of coffee.

END NOTES

1.   *United States v. Kokinda*, 497 U.S. 720 (1990).
2.   See *Lamb's Chapel v. Center Moriches Union Free School District*, 113 S.Ct. 2141 (1993).
3.   *Hague v. Committee for Industrial Organization*, 307 U.S. 496, 515 (1939).
4.   *Id*, at 516.
5.   *Id.*
6.   *Forsythe County, Georgia v. Nationalist Movement*, 112 S.Ct. 2395 (1992).
7.   See, e.g., *Lovell v. City of Griffin*, 303 U.S. 444 (1938).
8.   *Kokinda*, 497 U.S. 720, 733-734 (1990).
9.   *Id.,* at 734.
10. *Id.*
11. *Schneider v. State*, 308 U.S. 147 (1939).
12. Id., at 162.
13. *Lamb's Chapel*, 113 S.Ct. 2141 (1993).
14. *Lynch v. Donnelly*, 465 U.S. 668 (1984); *Allegheny County v. American Civil Liberties Union, Greater Pittsburgh Chapter*, 492 U.S. 573 (1989).
15. *Lynch.*
16. *Allegheny County.*
17. *West Virginia v. Barnette*, 319 U.S. 624 (1943).
18. *Id.* at 642
19. *Westside Community Schools v. Mergens*, 496 U.S. 248 (1990).
20. *Tinker v. Des Moines Independent School District*, 393 U.S. 503 (1969).
21. *Id.,* 509.
22. *Tinker* at 506.
23. *Tinker* at 513.
24. *Lee v. Weisman*, 112 S.Ct. 2649 (1992).
25. *Id.* at 2655.
26. *Jones v. Clear Creek Independent School District*, 977 F.2d 963, 972 (5th Cir. 1992) (*Jones II*).
27. *Id., at 963.*
28. *Id.,* at 969 (citing *Mergens*, 496 U.S. 226, 250 (1990)).
29. *Harris v. Joint School District No. 241*, (Civ. No. 91-0166-N-HLR), (D. Idaho May 20, 1993) (post-*Lee* decision upholding the right of students to initiate prayers at graduation).
30. *Widmar v. Vincent*, 454 U.S. 263, 269 (1981) (citing *Heffron v. International Society for*

Krishna Consciousness, Inc., 452 U.S. 640 (1981)); *Westside Community Schools v. Mergens,* 496 U.S. 226 (1990); *Niemotko v. Maryland,* 340 U.S. 268 (1951); *Saia v. New York,* 334 U.S. 558 (1948).

31. *Tinker,* 393 U.S. 503, 509 (1969).
32. *Widmar,* 454 U.S. 263 (1981).
33. *See Lamb's Chapel,* 61 U.S.L.W. 4549 (June 7, 1993).
34. *Tinker,* 393 U.S. 503, 512-13 (1969).
35. *Id.,* at 506.
36. *Mergens,* 496 U.S. at 248. *Lamb's Chapel,* 61 U.S.L.W. 4549 (June 7, 1993); *Grace Bible Fellowship, Inc. v. Maine School Admin. Dist. #5,* 941 F.2d 45 (1st Cir. 1991); *Gregoire v. Centennial School Dist.,* 907 F.2d 1366 (3d Cir.), *cert. denied,* 111 S.Ct. 253 (1990); *Concerned Women for America v. Lafayette County,* 883 F.2d 32 (5th Cir. 1989).
37. *Shumway v. Albany Co. School Dist. No. 1,* No. 93-CV-0153J (D.Wyo. filed June 9, 1993).
38. *Wallace v. Jaffree,* 472 U.S. 38 (1985).
39. *Id.* at 62 (Powell, J. concurring) (citation and footnote omitted).
40. *Id.,* at 40 n.1.
41. *Id.,* at 59-61.
42. *Id.,* at 59-61.
43. *Tinker,* 393 U.S. at 513 (quoting *Burnside* at 749).
44. *Id.*
45. *Perry Educ. Assoc. v. Perry Local Educators' Assoc.,* 460 U.S. 37, 45 (1983).
46. *Florey v. Sioux Falls School Dist.,* 619 F.2d 1311, 1317 (8th Cir. 1980).
47. *Id.,* at 1314.
48. *School District of Abington Township v. Schempp,* 374 U.S. 203 (1963).
49. *Id.* at 225.
50. *Stone v. Graham,* 449 U.S. 39, 42 (1980).
51. *Lamb's Chapel,* 61 U.S.L.W. 4549 (June 7, 1993).
52. *Id.,* at 4552.
53. *See Lynch v. Donnelly,* 465 U.S. 668, 675, 680 (1984).
54. Teen-Aid, 723 East Jackson, Spokane, WA 99207, 509/482-2868; Project Respect, P.O. Box 97, Golf, IL 60025-0097, 708/729-3298.
55. Letter reprinted from: *How Good is Your School?* by Sally D. Reed—National Council for Better Education, Capital Headquarters, Washington, D.C. 20070-0158
56. *Tinker,* 393 U.S. 503, 506 (1969).
57. *Mergens,* 867 F.2d 1076 (1989),
58. *Tinker,* at 509 (quoting *Burnside v. Byars,* 363 F.2d 744, 749 (5th Cir. 1966)).
59. *Tinker,* at 506.
60. *Id.,* at 512-13.
61. *Tinker,* at 511 (quoting *Burnside,* at 749).
62. *Id.,* at 509.
63. *Widmar v. Vincent,* 454 U.S. 263, 269 (1981) (citing *Heffron v. International Society for Krishna Consciousness, Inc.,* 452 U.S. 640 (1981)); *Westside Community Schools v. Mergens,* 496 U.S. 226 (1990); *Niemotko v. Maryland,* 340 U.S. 268 (1951); and *Saia v. New York,* 334 U.S. 558 (1948).
64. *Thomas v. Collins,* 323 U.S. 516, 537 (1945) (emphasis added)
65. *Widmar,* 454 U.S. 263 (1981)
66. *Garnett v. Renton School Dist. No. 403,* 987 F.2d 641 (9th Cir. 1993)
67. *Westside Community Schools v. Mergens,* 496 U.S. 226 (1990)
68. *Id.,* at 239-40.
69. *Id.* (quoting *McDaniel v. Paty,* 435 U.S. 618, 641 (1978) (Brennan, J., concurring in judg-